Towards Cohesive Local Government - Town and County

BAILE ÁTHA CLIATH:
ARNA FHOILSIÚ AG OIFIG AN tSOLÁTHAIR.
Le ceannach díreach ón
OIFIG DHÍOLTA FOILSEACHÁN RIALTAIS, TEACH SUN ALLIANCE,
SRÁID THEACH LAIGHEAN, BAILE ÁTHA CLIATH 2.
nó tríd an bpost ó
FOILSEACHÁIN RIALTAIS, AN RANNÓG POST-TRÁCHTA,
4 - 5 BÓTHAR FHEARCHAIR, BAILE ÁTHA CLIATH 2.
(Teil: 01-6613111 - fo-líne 4040/4045; Fax: 01-4752760)
nó trí aon díoltóir leabhar.

DUBLIN:
PUBLISHED BY THE STATIONERY OFFICE.
To be purchased directly from the
GOVERNMENT PUBLICATIONS SALE OFFICE, SUN ALLIANCE HOUSE,
MOLESWORTH STREET, DUBLIN 2.
or by mail order from
GOVERNMENT PUBLICATIONS, POSTAL TRADE SECTION,
4 - 5 HARCOURT ROAD, DUBLIN 2.
(Tel: 01-6613111 - ext. 4040/4045; Fax: 01-4752760)
or through any bookseller.

Price: £8.00

Report of Reorganisation Commission
April 1996

Contents

Appendices

Overview by the Chairman

We embarked on our review of town local government facing contrasting demands which seemed difficult to reconcile. On one side, there were aspirations for enhancement on the part of town authorities; on the other, an obligation to safeguard the position of the county councils as the primary units of local government and to ensure overall effectiveness, efficiency and economy.

We have sought, not only to balance these interests, but also to introduce fresh approaches to help avoid the sort of impasse which these issues have tended to reach. As our work progressed the more fundamental importance of issues such as the need to maximise the effectiveness of the total resources of local government, town and county, and to provide the best possible standard of service to the public, became clearly evident.

These issues have strongly influenced our approach and led us to identify as key objectives:

- greater cohesiveness between town and county authorities;

- customer service as a central factor in the way the local government system is organised and operated;

- the need to base the future role of town authorities on their particular strengths and capacities so that they can concentrate on what they are best fitted to do; and

- the need to accommodate diversity so that local arrangements can be designed to suit local circumstances rather than having to be fitted into a rigid, centrally-determined mould.

The structure of this report reflects these objectives. The future role of town authorities is considered in Part 2, with particular emphasis on the need to chart new directions for town authorities, while determining their most appropriate role in the more traditional areas. In Part 3 we recommend structural arrangements for the success of town local government in the future. Part 4 points out the arrangements - organisational, operational and financial - needed to underpin the proposed future role and structures and the various linkages which we consider a modern, cohesive and customer-oriented local service requires.

The report contains extensive recommendations and conclusions across the range of matters examined in the course of our review. These need to be considered primarily in the context of the relevant issues, as outlined in the appropriate chapters of the report. The following is a brief overview of the main points which emerge:

- In order to maximise overall effectiveness and quality of public service and to sustain the role envisaged for town authorities, there needs to be a far more integrated approach between town and county authorities. At operational level, there will be a joint staff and organisational structure, subject to deployment by the manager. There also needs to be increased linkage between elected members, including a structured system of meetings between town and county members.

- The integrated approach proposed should lead to the development of joint services centres, through merger of county council area offices with town authorities, where possible. These centres would provide convenient, customer-oriented service to the public for transaction of business with town and county authorities alike.

- There will be a single classification of town authorities, all to be titled "Town Council" with an office of "Mayor". There will, however, be scope for diversity rather than rigid definition of functions nationally on the basis of legal classification. Each authority can reach its own level of activity within broad parameters having regard to its capacity and to local circumstances and arrangements. There will be special provision for town councils which were formerly town commissioners to give them a meaningful future role.

- Wide scale creation of new town authorities is neither warranted nor feasible. Towns with population of 7,500 or over will be eligible for local authority status through appropriate procedures and subject to rigorous assessment of need and implications.

- Non local authority towns will have improved accessibility to and interaction with, the local government system, including a process of linkage with the county council and formal recognition of local voluntary associations, such as community councils.

- The role of town authorities needs to develop in new directions, with particular emphasis on representational, development and community-related aspects. This role must be concentrated on the particular strengths of town authorities, taking account also of their limitations and the requirements of operational effectiveness and quality of service.

- Town development and improvement should be a priority for town authorities in the future. This can range from traditional activities such as improvement of the physical appearance and general environment of local areas, to development activities on a broader front, such as tourism promotion, amenities and general development, with emphasis on support for local initiatives. A joint town improvement programme is proposed to provide a framework for co-ordination and input by both town and county authorities.

- Town authorities can be a key focus of civic and community leadership with an increased role in social and community development, particularly in supporting local initiatives and complementing the work of other agencies.

- An appropriate and flexible role is proposed for town authorities in the more traditional infrastructural and regulatory areas, having regard to current needs and the organisational and other changes proposed, as follows:

  Housing will continue to be an important community related-function for town local authorities but there is need for closer co-operation and more integrated arrangements.

  In *Planning,* town authorities can operate with county council support and provide a suitable structure for public participation.

  Local Roads functions, given their significance to town authority operations, should be retained but with more integrated local operational arrangements which need to be kept under review.

  Water Services are an important element of overall environmental functions which generally involve a context well beyond town areas; a more effective water resources management system can be achieved through full integration of the water services and water pollution control systems at county level.

- Because town and county authorities are separate revenue-raising bodies there are potentially serious financial difficulties with a major programme of boundary extensions which, cumulatively, could adversely affect county council finances and organisation in the long run. Circumstances in which there may be scope for change in the short term are limited. Any general programme of extensions should await the introduction of a more unified revenue-raising system. This matter should be looked at as part of the review of local authority finance.

- Town authority involvement in local development and other community-related activities should be underpinned by structured linkage with local communities, including joint meetings with representatives of appropriate local groups.

- There needs to be an effective overall framework for implementation of reform and a process to keep the development of local government under review in the longer term.

The above points give a foretaste of the main thrust of our conclusions. We believe that, within the parameters of our review which require, in particular, retention of all existing town authorities, we have arrived at an approach which will promote the fundamental objectives of effectiveness and public service. This approach balances the aims of democratic representation and operational efficiency, providing a suitable, meaningful role for all town authorities, with particular emphasis on the role of the elected members both as representatives of, and leaders of, their communities.

We have been particularly helped and influenced by the wide range of submissions made to us by individuals and bodies, both within and outside of local government. We acknowledge our appreciation of these, particularly those who took the time and trouble to meet us and give us the benefit of their knowledge and experience. We wish to record our particular gratitude to a group of local authority officials, Mr Ned O'Connor, Tipperary South County Council, Mr Tony Davis, Louth County Council and Mr Willie Wixted, Tralee UDC, who gave us valuable assistance, particularly in assessment of the impact of possible structural changes. For an account of local government in Wales and its recent reorganisation, we are grateful to Mr. Huw James, Pembrokeshire County Council who attended one of our meetings.

Acknowledgements in a report of this kind often tend to be a simple matter of form. In this case that would be quite inappropriate. We wish to record our appreciation for the support we have received in our work from our Secretary, Denis Conlan who made an outstanding contribution. We could not have dealt with the range of material and issues without his sterling service. We extend our thanks also to his colleagues who helped in the preparation of material, organisation of meetings, typing and production of this report and providing excellent general support to the Commission.

I would like to record my deep appreciation to the members of the Commission - Margaret Adams, Gretta Cronin, Kevin Cullen, Seamus Dooley, Michael O'Brien and Anne O'Keeffe for their dedication and commitment to the task. It was my privilege and pleasure to work with such an excellent group and I have fond memories of the time we spent together.

I have pleasure in submitting the Report to the Minister for the Environment in accordance with statutory requirements. To a significant extent, however, it calls for action on the part of local authorities and this will be crucial to the future success of town local government.

Jim Lacey,
Chairman,
Local Government Reorganisation Commission.
April, 1996

Part

I

Background
and
Approach

Chapter 1

General Context

This chapter outlines briefly the main issues and developments leading to the present review.

Establishment of commission

1.1   A Government statement of 27 January, 1994, indicated that local government would be reorganised at the sub-county level. No existing town authorities were to be abolished and elections to those authorities (postponed since 1985) would be held in June, 1994, on the basis of the built up town area. An independent statutory commission was proposed to carry out a review of sub-county local government. The Local Government Act, 1994, provided for this and the review began in early 1995. The Commission members are: Mr. James Lacey (Chairman); Councillor Margaret Adams; Ms. Gretta Cronin; Mr. Kevin Cullen; Mr. Seamus Dooley; Councillor Michael O'Brien; Ms. Anne O'Keeffe.

1.2   The Commission's task was to draw up an appropriate modern framework for the eighty existing town authorities with recommendations for their structural, functional, staffing, financial and other organisational arrangements. The Commission was also to consider the implications of any proposals for county councils as the primary units of local government, the relationship between the town and county authorities and criteria and procedures for the possible establishment of new town authorities.

Previous reports

1.3   The question of sub-county local government structures has been on the agenda for at least twenty-five years and has been examined in the course of various reviews of local government, giving rise to a number of reports or policy documents. Relevant aspects of these are summarised in Chapter 4.

1.4   The various reviews were undertaken against the background of widespread recognition that the existing system of town local authorities was unsatisfactory in certain respects such as: a multiple classification of sub-county authorities which is not meaningful or rational - three different categories of town authorities (boroughs, urban district councils (UDCs) and town commissioners) each containing towns of varying size, while some other centres of population do not have a separate town authority; the fact that the town commissioners are archaic and almost powerless; mismatch between capacity and nominal functions in many cases, with town functions frequently being discharged in practice by or through the county councils; inappropriate infrastructural responsibilities which require a larger than town scale and a range of professional and technical expertise not available to towns; physical expansion of many towns beyond their administrative boundaries; lack of a geographically comprehensive tier of sub-county territorial units - the town authorities are isolated entities within the counties; a legal framework which was confusing, inconsistent and outdated in many respects.

Polarised debate

1.5 Debate on reform of sub-county local government has often tended to be polarised. The need to balance the objective of administrative efficiency and economy with that of ensuring adequate structures of democratic representation has been problematic. While the former could suggest a county or larger scale, with the abolition of small authorities and a revision of the legal powers of others, small units are often seen as inherently more democratic; and existing structures have come to be regarded as almost sacrosanct. The possibility of structural rationalisation, or indeed of other changes, has been an emotive issue, particularly among members of town authorities, over a long period. The Barrington Committee report in 1991 (see Chapter 4), while agreeing that the town system in its existing form was inherently unsatisfactory and incapable of resolution by a general extension of town boundaries, failed to produce an agreed recommendation on the matter. Instead, two widely divergent options were proposed for sub-county structures - either elected district councils or district committees of county councils with local community linkage. The Government of the time considered that further examination of the matter was necessary and town elections were again postponed by the Local Government Act, 1991, pending further legislation.

Recent reforms

1.6 The Commission's review of town local government represents the latest phase of a programme of local government reform pursued by successive governments since 1990, involving the enactment of three Local Government Acts and the implementation of various reforms under those Acts, including a range of provisions relating to the structure of local government. Structural reorganisation of local government in the Dublin area involving the establishment of three new county councils was provided for in the Local Government (Dublin) Act, 1993. The role and status of the county and city councils as the primary units of local government in Ireland was formally affirmed in the Local Government Act, 1994, reflecting the approach followed by successive Governments. A new statutory regional level for co-ordination purposes was added to the Irish local government system with the establishment of eight regional authorities in 1994. The reorganisation and reform of sub-county structures thus remained as an outstanding issue now being addressed in this review.

A Government of Renewal

1.7 The current Government's policy agreement, *A Government of Renewal*, published in December, 1994, stated that "structures and funding will be put in place to return the greatest amount of opportunities to an effective and accountable local administration". It went on to state that a professional study would be undertaken to see how a fair, equitable and reasonable system of local government finance can be introduced. A Devolution Commission was also proposed to oversee a phased programme of devolution which would observe the principle of subsidiarity and widen the role of local government so that local authorities would become the focus for local development and for the co-ordination of various other local development structures. Both the study of local government finance and the Devolution Commission review were initiated in 1995 and are currently under way.

The review in context

1.8 The statutory terms of reference constrained this review more tightly as to possible options than previous ones (see 2.5 and 2.6). The terms of reference, the scope and objectives of the Commission's review and the approach taken in the light of these are discussed further in Chapter 2. The recommendations in this report must be considered against the background of our terms of reference. We are also mindful of the possible implications of the reviews of local government finance and devolution referred to above which could have a significant bearing on certain aspects of reform of town local government. Certain issues referred to further in this report will need to be considered in the context of those reviews. However, most of the recommendations in this report are capable of implementation within the existing local government system or in the context of any adjustments which might arise from the other reviews.

Chapter 2

Scope of Review

This chapter outlines the implications for the Commission's review of its statutory terms of reference, the structures of the local government system and other concurrent studies.

Local government and towns

2.1 There are, in all, 114 directly elected local authorities in the State in five legal classes. There are 34 city or county councils and 80 towns; each with a separate directly elected town local authority - borough corporation, urban district council or town commissioners. These towns are located within and form part of their relevant counties[1]. The town authorities and their relationships with the county councils are the main subject of this review. Other towns do not have separate town authorities, an aspect which is dealt with in Chapter 10.

2.2 Information on local government structures is contained in Chapter 9 which deals with the system of town classification. A general outline of the local government system is given at Appendix 1 and data for each of the 114 elected local authorities are at Appendix 2.

2.3 According to the report on the 1991 Census the populations of local authority towns range in size from 459 to 25,843 within their existing administrative boundaries. The town commissioners exercise a mainly representational role with almost no service responsibilities, while the other authorities are responsible for a varying range of services within the town (e.g. housing, roads, water, planning, amenities, etc.). The total population of these 80 towns within the existing administrative boundaries is 473,000 or about 13% of the total population of the State. If the full environs[2] population (105,403)[3] of these towns is added it would bring the total to about 16% of the State population. The combined populations of the towns with separate town authorities represents 17% of the total county populations (i.e. excluding the five cities) and if all town environs are included this figure increases to 21%. The towns have a total of 744 elected members compared with a total of 883 representatives for city and county authorities. The town authorities have a total estimated current expenditure of £102m (1996) - 8% of total local authority current expenditure; capital expenditure of £73m (1994 outturn) and a total staff of 2,216 at 31 December, 1994 (out of an overall local authority total of about 30,000).

Terms of reference

2.4 The Commission's terms of reference are contained in sections 55 and 56 of the Local Government Act, 1994. The provisions of the Act relating to the review of town local government are set out in Appendix 3.

---

[1] There are no town local authorities in some counties (Leitrim, Limerick, Dun Laoghaire-Rathdown, South Dublin) and only town commissioners in others (Laois, Roscommon).

[2] Environs are that part of the continuous built up town outside of the legally defined administrative area. They are defined, in accordance with international criteria, by the Central Statistics Office for Census purposes.

[3] This figure and subsequent population percentages include cross-county environs.

2.5 Section 56 of the 1994 Act sets out the matters on which the Commission must submit proposals. These are summarised as follows:

- arrangements for satisfactory local government for towns;

- the number of classes of town local authority and the class to which each existing town local authority should be assigned;

- the general role and functions appropriate to each class and financial, staffing and organisational matters;

- consequential implications for county councils and appropriate relationships between each class of town authority and county councils;

- appropriate criteria and procedures for establishment of local authorities in towns which currently do not have a separate local authority;

- any other relevant matters relating to local government and measures and arrangements for implementation of proposals.

2.6 Section 55 of the 1994 Act sets out matters to which the Commission must have regard in preparing its report including:

- the need to secure maximum benefit from the operation of the local government system;

- representation of local community interests;

- the need for effectiveness, efficiency and economy and the best use of available resources;

- the need to safeguard the position of county councils as the primary units of local government;

- the need to ensure that there is no avoidable increase in financial demands on the Exchequer or local authorities or in staff numbers and costs;

- community identity, civic tradition, local capabilities and capacities;

- provision of a proper system of local government for towns consistent with the foregoing paragraphs;

- submissions to the Commission.

2.7 These provisions place relatively tight constraints on the options available to the Commission in formulating its recommendations. For example, unlike previous reviews the Commission did not have freedom to consider any fundamental rationalisation at sub-county level. Each existing town authority is to be retained within the future classification system. At the same time, the Commission's proposals must provide for safeguarding the position of county councils as the primary units of local government and have regard to the need for effectiveness, efficiency and economy and to ensure there is no avoidable increase in financial demands which fall ultimately on the taxpayer. These requirements have somewhat conflicting implications and their combined effect narrows the range of options open to the Commission.

Contrasting views

2.8 Differing approaches to reorganisation and to priorities are evident in submissions made to the Commission (to which it is statutorily obliged to have regard) and there is a range of aspirations, such as: desire of most town authorities for an enhanced role; administrative boundary extensions in towns where electoral areas were changed in 1994; general desire for additional resources. There are also aspirations for the creation of new town authorities for certain towns which do not currently have a separate town authority. At the same time, concern was expressed on the part of county councils about possible implications of such structural changes, particularly for the capacity to provide adequately for the future needs and development of the county as a whole, including the needs of certain towns which depend significantly on assistance from the county council. The obligation on the Commission to ensure that there is no avoidable increase in financial demands or staff numbers or costs was a further crucial factor in considering proposals made to it.

Existing structural realities

2.9 As well as the statutory limitations within which it must work, the Commission's options were also conditioned by certain current structural realities. The profile of town local authorities is outlined at Appendix 2. Ireland has a relatively weak urban structure by international comparison; only ten local authority towns (i.e. excluding the five cities) have a population of 15,000 or more, even with the inclusion of environs outside of the administrative boundaries. A significant number of local government towns underwent population decline or remained relatively static in the 1986 - 1991 inter-censal period. Population growth was largely confined to some cities, towns within their zones of influence and a very limited number of other centres.

2.10 A particular feature of Irish sub-county structures is that the town authorities are isolated units within the counties separated from their natural hinterlands. In contrast, the norm throughout Europe is for a comprehensive territorial division at the lower tier. For example in France, each Département is fully subdivided into Communes. Among the advantages of the latter structure is that it facilitates inter-authority co-operation and aggregation in the discharge of certain functions and so allows for operational units of reasonable size, thus increasing the operational viability for some purposes of even some relatively small units. Such horizontal interaction is generally not feasible within the present Irish sub-county model, thus reducing the possibility of benefiting from economies or efficiencies of scale.

2.11 Many town authorities originated in the medieval era of chartered walled towns. With modern communications, the towns, especially the larger centres, exert a significant role as the focus of much wider hinterlands. Consequently, a local government model based on the concept of isolated town units does not always reflect current social and economic realities. For example, travel to work patterns, school transport catchment areas, shopping catchment areas and the overall pattern of economic and social interaction in the modern era bear little relationship to current structures or boundaries. In this context it is noteworthy that most of the local development structures[4] established outside of the local government system in recent years operate at county level or on a scale significantly larger than towns; none are confined solely to town boundaries.

2.12 The scope for enhancement of many town authorities is also influenced by the scale of their existing organisation and operations. In considering the possibilities for upgrading town authority powers and functions, regard must be had to the fact that even some towns which, by Irish standards, have relatively large populations, currently have local authorities of only minimal organisational and operational scale. The financial and other resource implications of possible upgrading must also be considered, both in absolute terms and in relation to the position of the county councils. This point applies with equal and possibly greater force in relation to the question of possible establishment of new town local authorities. The question of possible impact on county councils has a further dimension in terms of disparities within the county system. In some smaller and less well-resourced counties, the significance of towns relative to the overall scale and resources of the county as a whole is much greater than in larger counties. This is manifested, for example, in the fact that in some counties a few towns account for a high proportion of the total commercial valuation for rating purposes. In contrast, the limited resource base available in certain towns must also be considered. It is also noteworthy that there is a significant disparity between the functions legally or nominally available to many existing urban district councils and the extent to which such functions are actually fully discharged by such authorities in their own right. The question of limited capacity applies a fortiori to many existing town commissioners.

Related studies

2.13 The final factor outside of the Commission's control, but having potentially significant implications for the ultimate effects of its recommendations, is the fact that there are concurrently two major reviews in progress, one on local government finance and the other on the question of devolution of functions from central level to local government and linkage of local government with the recently established local development structures. These issues are referred to at relevant points in this report. Attention is drawn to certain issues which arose in the course of the review which would appear to warrant further examination in the context of the other reviews. Generally, however, the Commission formulated its recommendations on the basis of the existing system of local government financing and current range of functions, while recognising, however, that adaptations may arise in the light of the outcome of the other reviews.

---

[4] 35 County Enterprise Boards; 36 LEADER Groups; 38 Area Partnership Companies

An improved town system

2.14 Notwithstanding constraints, the Commission considers that significant improvements can be effected in the aspects of the local government system which are within the scope of its review. We have, accordingly, sought to achieve the most positive and productive results for town local government. At the same time we have also sought to promote the good of the local government system as a whole and above all, the benefit of the public who are ultimately the customers of the local government service, whether provided by town or county authorities. It is important not to view town local government in isolation from the county level or indeed from other local structures but rather as an integral element of the overall local service. This approach, and above all the objectives of service to the public and overall effectiveness, are guiding principles throughout this report.

2.15 This is the first review focussed primarily on town local government - a phrase used throughout the report to refer to town local authorities generally i.e. borough corporations, urban district councils and town commissioners (subject to specific references, particularly in relation to the latter). The report's specific focus on "towns" and town-related matters does not imply any less priority attaching to other areas. It merely reflects the specific statutory remit of the Commission as part of an overall programme of local government reform which has been ongoing in recent years. Enhancement of town local government is likely to benefit the wider hinterlands which towns serve and the local government system as a whole. Furthermore, most of the recommendations in this report would be equally valid and applicable, subject to suitable modification, to alternative sub-county structures.

Chapter 3

The Commission's Approach

This chapter provides a general outline of the Commission's methodology and the main features of the review.

General approach

3.1 The methodology followed by the Commission involved: a study of the existing system and its perceived problems and needs; review of issues and options raised in previous local government reviews; reference to relevant aspects of local government systems in other countries; consideration of submissions and formulation of recommendations in the light of the foregoing. We sought to follow a structured approach, focussing on key aspects such as the appropriate role of town local government, the structural, organisational and financial framework needed for effective discharge of town authority functions and measures to improve the quality of service to the public. We held a total of 18 Commission meetings aside from consultations with various groups (see Appendix 4).

The present system

3.2 The Commission's point of departure was to examine the existing system of town local government with particular reference to structures, functions, financial arrangements, staffing and organisation. The main features of the present system are set out in Appendix 1 and Appendix 2 in order to provide a convenient factual background.

Previous studies

3.3 The Commission considered it important to have regard to relevant issues in previous reports and statements on local government reform and reorganisation, although noting that some options considered in these are not available to the Commission because of its terms of reference. The main points relevant to the review of town local government contained in previously published documents are set out in Chapter 4.

Submissions and consultations

3.4 As required by the 1994 Act, the Commission publicly invited written submissions for consideration in the context of its review. The Commission also wrote individually to each local authority inviting them to make submissions. By the closing date of 31 March, 1995, a total of 80 written submissions had been received. A further 41 written submissions were received after that date and these were also fully considered. Consideration of submissions formed a key element of the review, with particular reference to views expressed by local authorities and local authority members' associations. A wide range of issues were raised in submissions, outlining perceived problems, aspirations, strengths and weaknesses of town local government. On some points, however, it was noted that generalised suggestions or desires rather than specific proposals tended to predominate. Equally, there was quite wide divergence of opinion on certain issues.

3.5 Time constraints precluded comprehensive oral consultations. However, the Commission met with a representative selection of town authorities as apart of its fact finding work and to obtain a deeper insight into the significant issues affecting town local government. Priority was given to meeting representatives of the elected members of the town authorities, but in conjunction with these meetings we also had discussions with county council representatives and relevant managers/assistant managers and town clerks. We also met with delegations from the Association of Municipal Authorities of Ireland and the General Council of County Councils. We placed considerable importance on the views of these bodies as the national representative organisations of the elected members of the respective sets of local authorities. We also met a delegation from the Association of City and County Managers. We had a joint meeting with representatives of a small number of non-local government community groups who had requested meetings.[1] Their input is particularly appreciated given the voluntary nature of their work and lack of back-up resources.

3.6 Some of the features noted above in relation to written submissions were also manifested in the oral consultations, particularly divergence of opinions and lack of specific proposals for the attainment of certain stated objectives. Nonetheless, we found these meetings extremely valuable in providing elaboration on matters raised in written submissions, deeper understanding of local concerns and priorities and bringing to attention certain additional issues. We wish to record our gratitude and appreciation to all who took the time, trouble and effort to provide information or views to us. These submissions provided an important platform for the development of recommendations and the general thrust of the report is informed and significantly influenced by them. Particular matters raised are referred to at relevant points in this report and a full list of persons and groups who made written or oral submissions is given at Appendix 4.

Formulation of recommendations

3.7 In the light of its examination of the existing system of town local government, relevant matters raised in previous reports and the submissions made to it, the Commission identified particular goals which its recommendations should seek to attain within the overall objective of satisfactory local government for towns and the more specific requirements and parameters of the 1994 Act. These are:

- to ensure that the local government service as a whole is organised and operates in a cohesive manner to deliver the best possible standard of service and representation to the people, having regard to available resources;

- to enable town authorities to develop to their maximum potential and make the best possible contribution to the delivery of local services, with effective and efficient interaction between them and county councils;

---

[1] Cahir Development Association, Celbridge Community Council, Kildare Town Twinning Association, Malahide Community Council Ltd.

- to facilitate the most productive relationships between local authorities and individuals or groups locally;

- to design a system which is flexible enough to accommodate diversity in local circumstances while at the same time securing due compatibility with and support for national plans, policies and objectives;

- to ensure that the Commission's recommendations will be practicable and implementable; and

- to ensure that sufficient account is taken of possible implications for the review of local government finance and the Devolution Commission review.

Chapter 4

Previous Reports

This chapter gives a brief synopsis of material relevant to town local government in reports and policy documents published in relation to the reform of local government structures and functions during the past 25 years.

Local Government Reorganisation, **White Paper, 1971:**

4.1 The White Paper was presented to both Houses of the Oireachtas in February, 1971. Its general comments regarding sub-county local government included the following:

The existing classification of town authorities is based on historical factors rather than logical principles. Smaller authorities do not have the financial and organisational resources available to them to discharge their functions effectively and to play an active role in the development of their areas, and there is little logic in confining responsibility (including financial responsibility) for development of the towns to their residents since many people resident outside avail of their amenities. The transfer of functions of many urban authorities to county level was proposed to facilitate the development of the towns concerned, to achieve financial and organisational improvements and to spread the burden of expenditure over all those who avail of the amenities of the town.

The main recommendations relevant to town local government include the following:

- Local government would be based primarily on the county, subject to some boundary adjustment and increased co-operation and joint action.

- Due to limited resources and insufficient statutory powers, town commissioners and small urban authorities would be abolished and functions transferred to county councils but this need not preclude continuance of the status of the towns concerned "for ceremonial and other traditional purposes".

- New arrangements within counties in place of small town authorities; to involve area committees of county councils (consisting of councillors, representatives of local development associations and other bodies concerned with the economic, social and cultural development of the area) with minor functions related to local needs delegated to them.

- Local offices of the county council would deal with local services (e.g. house repairs, local road maintenance, rent/rate collection, planning applications) and provision of customer services (e.g. information, queries, complaints) which could be extended gradually to include other public services.

- Proposed changes in structures would affect staffing - appropriate consultation together with further reviews would be undertaken arising from transfer to county councils of responsibility for many urban areas.

- Development of community councils with links to the local government system would be encouraged and existing provisions regarding approved local councils amended.

- Separate elected councils with a comprehensive range of functions would be retained in suitable towns (determined on the basis of existing size, population, resources and local views - special machinery to be established to assess these factors) involving a new single class of urban authority in place of borough corporations and urban district councils in places which are to retain a separate authority.

- Boundaries of retained town authorities would be updated to take in built environs and a 20-year development belt.

- Special arrangements to ensure co-ordination of policies and activities of town authorities with those of county councils including the sharing of specialist staff.

- General updating and rationalisation of local government law; rationalisation of miscellaneous functions; reduction in unnecessary controls and improved accounting and audit arrangements; updating of provisions relating to constitution, membership and procedures of local authorities; repeal of charters of borough corporations.

- Enhanced development role for local authorities.

Local Government Reorganisation, Discussion Document, 1973:

4.2   The discussion document was published by the Minister for Local Government in December, 1973. The following are the main proposals of relevance to sub-county local government:

- County councils to remain as the principal local authorities.

- Existing town commissioners and urban district councils (UDCs) to be retained.

- Redistribution of functions between classes of local authorities (due to insufficient resources of urban authorities) as follows:

    - *planning and development:* transfer to county council (with the exception of larger designated urban areas) but urban authorities to have a consultative role in connection with the development plan, and a right of appeal;

- *housing*: flexible power to transfer functions relating to house construction of all or specified urban authorities (including boroughs) to county councils; urban authorities to retain other functions such as assessment of needs, allocation of tenancies and rent collection; urban authorities to submit a housing policy for their area to county council; operation of various housing grants/loans by county councils in respect of all urban districts and boroughs; all remaining housing functions of town commissioners to transfer to county councils;

- *sanitary services*: transfer to county council but urban authorities to have power to make representations and right of appeal in the event of conflict.

• UDCs to retain existing roads/traffic functions within their areas.

• County councils to provide staffing services to urban authorities.

• Simplified procedures for establishment of new authorities with limited, mainly representational, functions.

• Legislation to provide a simplified and comprehensive boundary adjustment process.

• Law relating to constitution, membership, civic activities, procedures and committees of local authorities to be modernised and simplified.

• Extension of title of Mayor to UDCs, town commissioners and any new authorities.

• Possibility of county council levying rates in urban area to be the subject of further consideration.

• Local authority powers to be widened and central controls removed.

The Reform of Local Government, Policy Statement 1985:

4.3 The Policy Statement was issued by the Minister for the Environment in May, 1985, outlining Government proposals for local government reorganisation. The main points of relevance to town local government are summarised as follows:

• A new category of local authority - town council - for towns with population of 2,000 or more to replace existing town commissioners: town councils not to have executive functions in relation to works or services; their role will be to represent social and economic interests of the town community, to promote works of a community, recreational or amenity nature, to encourage initative within the community and provide a forum to discuss local needs and make them known to outside bodies.

- Simplified procedure to enable larger town councils to upgrade to UDC status.

- Provision for county councils to delegate responsibility for local works and services to town councils.

- Independent boundary commission to review urban boundaries.

- Improved framework to facilitate co-operation or joint provision of services, including extension of provisions relating to joint committees, provision of staffing services to other authorities and more flexible agency arrangements.

Local Government Reorganisation and Reform - Report of Advisory Expert Committee, 1991:

4.4 The report of the Committee, chaired by Dr. T.J. Barrington (hence commonly referred to as the *Barrington Report*) was published in March, 1991. The main proposals relevant to sub-county local government are summarised as follows:

- The local government system should be structured on three levels: regional, county and sub-county.

- County councils to be the executing authorities for major capital works programmes, services which need a county scale and for all staffing (one staff complement with appropriate staff allocated to districts, the county manager having overall responsibility).

- As regards town authorities the following problems were identified:

    - towns per se do not provide a framework for a comprehensive sub-county tier;

    - the majority of towns have populations well below 15,000; separation of towns from hinterland population ignores modern living patterns; most boundaries are outdated; incidence of town authorities throughout the country is haphazard;

    - limited statutory powers, staffing and financial resources;

    - mismatch of functions to capability of towns to discharge them efficiently;

    - functions allocated on the basis of legal status rather than capacity and capability of towns;

- Simply extending town boundaries to include environs and possibly future development areas, would not remedy problems but could fundamentally weaken the county system by reducing the latter's rating base without significantly improving town capability.

- For the foregoing reasons, sub-county arrangements need fundamental overhaul but the committee did not agree on a particular sub-county structure, presenting two different models, both involving replacement of existing town authorities - directly elected district councils or district committees of the county councils.

- While the two models differed significantly, in some respects common factors were identified, for example:

  - comprehensive sub-county territorial division,

  - the issue of non-viable town authorities addressed,

  - major infrastructural services to transfer to county councils.

- A boundary review group should be established and the law on boundary change updated.

- There should be structured arrangements to facilitate contact between local authorities and community groups and a contact officer designated for this purpose.

- The directly elected district council model would be largely dependent upon the degree of devolution of functions from central government and their establishment would depend on the emergence of a basic minimal level of functions which could be progressively built on.

- District councils would be responsible for: personal services in the district; co-ordination of services to ensure that they relate together to serve people's needs; general community development and co-operation with local voluntary groups; existing local government functions of particular local focus e.g. refuse collection, litter, small-scale amenity development, burial grounds, swimming pools, casual trading, minor road repairs, traffic control measures and aspects of various services which might be devolved to local government. Information technology should facilitate devolution of services to district level and decision-making should also devolve where appropriate.

Government Statement, 7 March, 1991:

4.5 This statement indicated the Government's decisions and proposals for a phased programme of local government reform in the light of the recommendations of the Barrington Committee. The main points of relevance to town local government were:

- The recommendation that the local government system should be structured on three levels was generally agreed.

- Failure of the Barrington Committee to agree on a sub-county structure was noted along with the fact that the divergent options would have radical effects - in one case almost doubling the number of councillors and the number of sub-county authorities, in the other the loss of separately elected authorities at sub-county level with a reduction of over 700 councillors; and in both cases, abolition of all existing sub-county authorities.

- The Government considered it necessary to examine the matter further as the reform programme developed, with a view to formulating acceptable and realistic sub-county structural arrangements.

- Various recommendations in the Barrington report relevant to both town and county authorities (e.g. general competence power, relaxation of controls on local authorities, enhancement of elected members' position, and updating of various legal aspects) to be dealt with in legislation (subsequently included in the Local Government Act, 1991).

Statement on Sub-County Local Government, 27 January, 1994:

4.6 This statement, issued by the Minister for the Environment announced details of decisions by the Government on local government reorganisation at sub-county level. The main points are summarised as follows:

- The existing town-based local authority system to be retained, but modernised and improved to reflect current realities.

- A statutory Reorganisation Commission to carry out a review and identify a modern framework for future municipal government.

- The Government rejected any suggestion that existing urban authorities be abolished or replaced by a new tier of district authorities.

- Town elections, postponed since 1985, to be held in June, 1994.

- A review of town areas so as to encompass built up environs, for electoral purposes only, to be implemented on the basis of local agreement in advance of the town elections.

- Authorities to continue their present functions and responsibilities within existing boundaries until appropriate transitional and consequential arrangements were worked out and implemented.

- The position of county councils as the primary units of local government to be safeguarded and financial effects of any changes to be satisfactory.

Statutory provision for the proposed review as well as for town authority elections and various other reforms was included in the Local Government Act, 1994.

Part
2

Future Role

Chapter 5

New Directions

The purpose of this chapter is to set out, within the Commission's terms of reference, a vision or philosophy of the future direction of town government and how the role of town authorities should develop, with particular emphasis on development of new roles beyond the traditional areas of local authority activity.

The role of local government

5.1 Local Government has a multi-faceted role featuring:

a *representational role* as an integral part of the democratic process, primarily involving elected members of local authorities as representatives of the people and as "trustees" of the local authority on their behalf, exercising the pre-eminent policy-making role and having general oversight and direction of the affairs of the authority;

an *operational role*, providing or securing the delivery of a range of services and execution of works, including the undertaking of projects in accordance with various national and EU programmes;

a *regulatory role*, involving statutory functions such as the issue of licences, permissions and similar authorisations and enforcement of, and monitoring compliance with, various legal codes;

a *community and general development role*, involving the formulation and implementation of plans, policies and measures to address problems and help improve generally the physical, economic and social character of the area and the general well-being of the community.

The administrative system to support these roles consists of the staff and other resources of local authorities together with essential financial, legal, procedural and electoral systems, and linkage with relevant non-local authority groups and agencies.

5.2 In order to chart the optimal future direction for town government it is necessary to consider the balance of emphasis as between these different roles. Traditionally local authorities in Ireland have been perceived mainly in terms of their operational activities and regulatory functions, and the public profile of their elected members. Local authorities have tended to be particularly associated with infrastructural works and services: housing, water and sewerage, roads; other facilities ranging from parks to traffic signs; delivery of important health or safety-related services such as refuse disposal and the fire service; performance of regulatory functions such as physical planning, building and environmental control; and revenue collection powers in relation to matters such as rates, motor taxation and service charges.

5.3 It is one of the Commission's objectives to define an appropriate role for town authorities within the traditional areas of activity and where appropriate, to recommend adjustments relevant to current circumstances. This aspect is dealt with in Chapter 8. However, in the light of its review, the Commission is satisfied that re-orientation of emphasis is called for both as regards the traditional areas and also as between them and the representational, development and promotional aspects referred to above.

Factors affecting the role of town local government

5.4 The following factors are particularly relevant to the development of the role of town authorities:

- The different categories of local authorities in Ireland do not constitute hierarchical tiers but rather separate geographically-based units. The urban authorities are largely independent entities located within the counties and do not generally have a direct functional relationship with the county based on subsidiarity or other relevant principles.

- In keeping with their largely separate status, the range of functions of town authorities (other than town commissioners) largely mirrors that of county councils, with the exception of certain matters confined to the latter. This arrangement carries an inherent risk of duplication and possibly even an element of unproductive competitiveness and defensiveness between the two levels. More significantly in the context of this review, it takes little or no account of the particular strengths and weaknesses of town authorities.

- An arrangement whereby the same degree of responsibility for a particular function is allocated to different levels of authority does not accord fully with a logical application of the principle of subsidiarity, whereby public services should be devolved to the lowest practicable level at which they can be discharged efficiently and effectively. This principle implies that, as far as possible, responsibility for a particular function should rest at a single level of authority.

- The broad multi-functional nature of local government has important strengths and advantages. It can, for example, be especially advantageous in mediating between competing objectives, reconciling conflicting effects or maximising the benefits of mutually complementary activities. This can be especially relevant in the infrastructural and development areas. In the case of smaller town authorities, however, a broad range of responsibilities can be a mixed blessing as the capacity and effectiveness of the authority may be strained in seeking to discharge a wide range of functions within a generally small operational scale, with necessarily finite resources and expertise. Greater return is likely to be obtained from concentrating the efforts and resources of smaller authorities on areas of activity in which they have what might be termed a comparative advantage.

- There is a risk of organisational and resource fragmentation by having responsibility for particular functions spread over a number of authorities within relatively confined geographical areas, but with such physical, organisational and legal separation as to militate against a cohesive approach.

- The fact that some of the traditional local authority functions, for example in the infrastructural, regulatory and emergency service areas, now require an operational, organisational, planning and funding scale of county, regional or, in some cases, national level, points to the need for re-orientation of the functions of town authorities to ensure that they continue to have a meaningful and substantial role. The Commission is satisfied that the need to locate different functions at different levels is wholly in accordance with the principle of subsidiarity. The key consideration insofar as town authorities are concerned is to define a role which is based solidly on their particular strengths and capabilities and the needs and priorities of their areas.

- The future shape and role of town local government must take account of changing needs and circumstances, including social, economic, demographic and technological developments, which may require new responses and a re-balancing of the traditional priorities. The desired flexibility and responsiveness on the part of local authorities to new demands and opportunities may be somewhat inhibited by an over-exclusive focus on long-standing functional compartments. An instance of the need for new responses is the increased focus on local development, with strong emphasis on local community initiative, area-based approaches and integration of action across different sectors.

- There is now a less rigid and uniform relationship between town authority classification and certain legal responsibilities (for example in the case of housing there is variation in the range of functions discharged by different urban authorities). New functions have also emerged, some of particular relevance to towns, such as urban renewal. Urbanisation has brought added emphasis and new dimensions to social and community issues.

- More specific account needs to be taken of local community activity and organisations. Issues which need to be addressed in this context include: the expectations of local communities for increased participation in and influence over decisions affecting them; the need to generate increased interest in and support for local government and to enhance public perception of local authorities.

- It is essential that the needs of the public are met in the most effective and efficient manner possible, with emphasis on quality and convenience of service, taking account of the high standards which the public are entitled to expect from public authorities.

- The future position of town authorities in the local government system must reflect the changes which have occurred in matters such as transportation, social and economic interaction and people's perspectives generally. It is no longer meaningful or realistic to regard town authorities in complete isolation from their wider hinterlands. Equally, account must be taken of how the town authorities relate to the internal organisational and operational divisions within the county council.

General principles for the future direction of town local government

5.5   In the light of the foregoing considerations, the Commission has identified certain principles which it feels should guide the definition of the future role of town local authorities and their position within the overall local service, as follows:

- There should be significantly increased emphasis on the development role of town authorities, including physical, social, economic, community and general development.

- A degree of re-orientation of emphasis is required from infrastructural functions to areas of activity which involve a significant element of engagement with the community, and matters which specifically relate to the welfare of the town and its citizens.

- The future role of town local authorities should be founded particularly on matters which involve a significant element of leadership, policy formulation and decision-making by the elected members.

- Positive, structured and inclusive partnership between local communities and the local authority is desirable. This should be a two-way process which, in one direction, will help to support and stimulate local initiative, and in the other, facilitate maximum awareness of, involvement and participation in and support, for local government affairs on the part of the community.

- There is need for improved modes of interaction between town and county authorities in areas such as organisation, resources and operational arrangements. Greater emphasis on co-ordination, co-operation and where appropriate, integration is needed. The objective is an effective and cohesive total local service.

- Provision of the highest possible quality service to the public is a fundamental objective. A new role should be developed for town and county authorities in this context, involving the provision of an integrated, comprehensive and user friendly local government service which facilitates convenient access for the public and elected members to information and services of all authorities within a county.

5.6   Town local government is a valuable part of the overall system of democracy and public administration.   If, its role is too narrowly confined, insufficiently attuned to current developments or based on functions which it is not best fitted to perform, it will be an underutilised resource with sub-optimal performance. The role of town local government must be sufficiently broad and flexible to enable it to meet new challenges and changing circumstances. Its structures, operations and relationships must be capable of supporting this role. We believe that the principles set out at 5.5 will help to achieve these objectives. These principles and issues arising from them, are reflected in more specific recommendations on the various matters which the Commission is required to address as outlined in succeeding chapters of this report.

Chapter 6

Town Development

This chapter deals with local authority activities extending beyond the traditional mainstream infrastructural and regulatory range. These involve various types of development; local projects, services and promotional work for improvement of the town and the community. These functions are formally in different local authority programme groups but together they form a significant element of the overall town authority role of promoting and fostering the development of their area, either directly or, as is increasingly the case, in partnership with others.

The importance of the development role

6.1   Demographic and transportation changes have contributed to a significant alteration in the role of many towns in the social and economic landscape of late twentieth century Ireland. Their role as centres of a wider hinterland has assumed increasing significance for social, educational, recreational, employment and commercial purposes. Equally, the contrasting trends of expanding population in some towns and relative stagnation or decline in others have created new demands. Consequently, functions relating to the development of towns merit particular attention in the context of the future role of town authorities. The term "development" is used in this chapter to cover a broad range of activities from minor amenities to projects of benefit to the local economy.

6.2   In recent years, local authorities have become increasingly involved, often in conjunction with other local interests, in development activities related to their traditional functions, such as the improvement of the physical appearance and general attractiveness of local areas and streetscapes and the provision of amenities. Alongside this, new local authority initiatives have emerged which are related more directly to development in the broadest sense, including matters such as enterprise support and promotion, enhancement of local tourism potential and general development measures for local areas and communities. Projects and activities of this nature may involve funding or other input from a variety of sources, including utilisation of FAS schemes, Community Employment Schemes, input from local bodies, partnership with commercial interests and a local authority role varying from that of lead actor to provision of support, encouragement and assistance for measures promoted by others.

6.3   We consider that activities of the sort referred to at 6.2 should be a key aspect in developing the role of town authorities in new directions, In line with the principles put forward in Chapter 5. This will involve bringing these functions to the forefront of the role of town authorities generally. There is a role for all types of town authority in the area of local improvement and development. The importance and scale of action in this area will vary depending on local circumstances and capabilities. In very many cases, it will involve active engagement with and participation by local community and other groups. This approach can facilitate progress which is beyond the reach of either a town authority, other public agency or local group acting alone. It will require the development of a shared sense of ownership, vision and civic solidarity among all of the participants, within a broadly based participatory process. The town authority can provide a focus for action. It can identify particular town needs and develop a coherent and cohesive strategy of town improvement. Recommendations are set out in succeeding paragraphs with a view to deepening and enhancing this role. An improved framework for action by and partnership between town and county authorities, and even more importantly, with local interests, is needed to advance the welfare and development of the towns and their communities.

General development functions

6.4 Local authorities, including town authorities, have a range of powers to promote the development of their areas, including the provision of sites and commercial and other facilities; tourism promotion and provision of tourist facilities; urban renewal; heritage and cultural activities; and other promotional work. Some of these derive from provisions of the 1963 Planning Act designed to underpin a new role envisaged for local authorities at that time as development corporations, in conjunction with their infrastructural functions. A more general permissive power to take action to promote the interests of the local community was conferred on all local authorities by the Local Government Act, 1991. This enables a local authority to engage in activities to promote the social, economic, environmental, recreational, cultural, community or general development of its area or community. Such activities may take many different forms, involving either direct action by local authorities or co-operation with and assistance to other parties. We recognise that the main strategic role in local authority development activity would rest with the county council. However, it is also desirable to establish a framework to facilitate participation by town authorities to whatever extent their capabilities permit, with particular emphasis on linkages with the county council and other bodies in a coherent overall strategy.

6.5 The capacity of town authorities to facilitate local development is conditioned to some extent by factors such as the extent of their operational scale, resource availability and functional remit. There is need to avoid duplication or wasteful competition with either the private sector or other public authorities (including county councils). The emergence in recent years of new special-purpose local development agencies, some based primarily on the generation and support of "bottom up" initiatives, others with a greater element of "top down" input, also has a bearing on this matter. However, new opportunities have opened for town authority participation in development, with the emphasis particularly on partnership. The urban renewal process over the past ten years provides clear evidence of the capacity of town authorities to play a valuable role in the physical and economic development of their areas. Town authorities can also make a significant direct contribution to physical development and indirectly contribute to economic development through the successful exercise of their traditional functions of housing, planning, roads and amenity provision. Moreover, measures taken by town authorities to improve the appearance, environment and amenities of their towns can, in addition to their intrinsic benefit to the local community, play a valuable role in areas of activity such as the promotion of tourism, attraction of industrial investment, encouragement of commercial ventures and other economic spin-offs.

6.6 Some town authorities have moved further than others in terms of direct involvement in promoting, assisting or undertaking development initiatives. Some have entered into commercial type operations and participated in joint ventures with local community or private sector interests. There may be potential for other town authorities to follow the example of those who have successfully undertaken initiatives of this type, with due care for the protection of public funds from undue risk. Other small authorities have been particularly successful, in co-operation with local commercial and community interests, in improving and upgrading the general appearance of the town, in activating local interests and in progressing an agreed programme of action.

Town improvement programme

6.7 A constraint on the potential of individual town authorities to promote development is likely to be capacity limitation, especially in smaller towns. There is also a risk that where town and county authorities seek to promote development separately, the overall effectiveness of their efforts will not be maximised.   A high degree of co-ordination and co-operation between town and county authorities is, therefore, essential. The Commission recommends that a town improvement programme should be drawn up jointly by the town and county authorities to facilitate this. The programme would provide a broad context for input by both authorities to town development, drawing together proposals under different programmes. The improvement programme proposed would not cut across other specific programmes or plans but could reflect relevant matters contained in them. It would, for example, incorporate proposals relating to the provision of amenities and facilities and other matters which are dealt with later in this chapter and would include roads-related matters as referred to in Chapter 8. The town improvement programme would indicate measures proposed for the town and the input to be made to them by the town authority, local community and other interests and the county council. The formulation of such programmes would be facilitated by enhanced interaction between elected members of town and county authorities, while the implementation of such measures would be facilitated by general operational integration. Recommendations in these areas are contained in Chapter 12.

6.8 The joint town improvement programme would be reviewed annually and updated as necessary, ideally in conjunction with the preparation of the annual estimates of both authorities concerned. A system of joint meetings between members of the town authority and county council area committees (recommended in Chapter 12) would provide an appropriate forum for this. The programme would be separate from the statutory development plan but would clearly need to take account of the provisions of the latter and also of proposals under the urban renewal tax incentive scheme and the urban and village renewal scheme. Town authorities have the primary role of promoting the urban renewal scheme in their areas, with the town clerk usually designated as co-ordinating officer to oversee promotion of the scheme. County councils have the function of preparing action plans, setting out proposed activities on a county-wide basis under the urban and village renewal programme. Within the action plan, proposals for individual towns require close consultation with the town authorities concerned. The town improvement programme now proposed should provide a means of giving the elected members of the town authorities a more structured avenue of input to these schemes, while also ensuring a co-ordinated area-based focus on all of the various proposals and activities relating to development of the town. Particular account should be taken of local interests in formulating the programme and of the possibilities for action designed to facilitate projects/activities sponsored by them which are in harmony with the general strategy for town development.

6.9 The proposed town improvement programme concept can apply also in the case of former town commissioners[1], with the elected members having a role in the development programme jointly with the county council. It was emphasised to the Commission in the course of its review that it is essential to avoid fragmentation and dilution of resources and effort where, for example, the county council is currently making good progress with the development of a town. While the county council is likely to continue to be the main source of development activity, the elected members of even the smaller town authorities should, in future, have an enhanced role by participating in the framing of the town improvement programme and helping to generate, through partnership with the county council and other interests, the input needed to achieve desired improvements.

6.10 The extent of financial input by town authorities will clearly depend on local needs and priorities and on the authority's revenue base. It is not our function to make specific recommendations in that regard. Where additional expenditure is considered warranted, the relevant authority will need to make provision for this. The proposed town improvement programme would provide an improved context for such decisions, with input from both town and county authorities. In this regard, it is evident that county councils generally recognise the value to their areas as a whole of developing the towns and have, in many cases, invested accordingly. The scope for obtaining local financial input for specific projects can also be explored. It was suggested to the Commission, in the course of its consultations with local authorities, that there is scope for authorities to seek, via public consultation, an element of local voluntary contribution towards the cost of new desirable local amenities or facilities, with co-financing by the town authority and the county council. This could help to prioritise local aspirations. The Commission has no way of gauging the degree of potential for this approach; but the success of various local community groups in developing facilities - including in some cases quite extensive enterprise centres as well as amenities and services - involving a significant element of local voluntary fund-raising, and the response to recent local development initiatives, suggest that it is at least worth providing for this. Success would clearly depend on worthwhile projects being selected and on the ability of the authority, members and officials, to devote imaginative effort to promotion. A framework for this approach should be drawn up. It could embrace either voluntary input or a more formal approach, such as ad hoc contribution for specific projects over a specified period which might apply both to the town and the wider area that would benefit e.g. the county electoral area. This matter is referred to further in Chapter 15 in the context of financial arrangements. Recommendations in Chapter 14 regarding the development of improved linkage between local authorities and community groups and other local bodies should help to facilitate such arrangements.

---

[1] All towns will, as we envisage it, have the title of Town Council, hence the reference here to "former town commissioners". (See 10.9)

Provision of amenities and facilities and related activities

6.11 The provision and operation of various public amenities and facilities, either directly by town authorities or in partnership with local groups, is central to their role in local and community development and would form an important element of the town improvement programme. The type of matters involved include the provision of sports, recreational, leisure, artistic and cultural facilities, civic improvements and environmental and heritage protection/improvement. A detailed list of the sort of amenities, facilities and services in question is set out in the Local Government Act, 1994. This list is reproduced for information at Appendix 5.

6.12 While many of the foregoing matters are part of the traditional local authority role, they have generally enjoyed less prominence than infrastructural or regulatory functions such as roads, housing or planning. We consider that the town authority role in these areas merits greater emphasis because:

- the activities in question are very relevant to the sort of overall role envisaged for town authorities, with particular reference to the future development of their towns and enrichment of community life;

- the improvement of local amenities and facilities and the visibility of such projects, can help to promote wider social and economic benefits in an area;

- the powers outlined are available to all town authorities, including those currently in the town commissioner category; these matters do not, in many cases, involve high cost or complexity and each authority can tailor the scale of its activity in this regard to the level of its resources and capacity;

- the type of activities involved lend themselves well to development through co-operative arrangements between local authorities and through partnerships with local community and other interests;

- there appears to be insufficient awareness of the extent of powers available to town authorities in this area.

6.13 It is important that investment in the provision of amenities is approached on a co-ordinated or co-operative basis by town and county authorities, with agreed joint input where necessary. The concept of a joint town improvement programme already suggested should provide a suitable framework for this approach. If the existing legal framework is not considered sufficiently flexible to allow for this type of joint responsibility, the relevant provisions should be suitably adapted (this matter is considered further in Chapter 8 in the context of infrastructural functions). It is also important that community interests and relevant local groups are involved as fully as possible. Proposals in Chapter 14 for greater linkage between local authorities and community groups are relevant in this context.

Tidy towns

6.14 An area of activity closely related to town development and improvement is the annual Tidy Towns competition in which the Regional Tourism Organisations also play an important role. Some local authorities have traditionally played a significant role in assisting and promoting local involvement in the competition which, in turn, provides a special focus for local efforts to improve the environment in various ways and complements local authority activities in areas such as urban renewal, environmental improvement and general development. In 1995, responsibility for the Tidy Towns competition transferred from Bord Failte to the Department of the Environment. A review of the competition has since been undertaken which gives attention to the mutual complementarity between the tidy towns effort and the other activities and functions of town authorities.

6.15 The role of all town authorities in the Tidy Towns competition can be enhanced without, of course, in any way diminishing or compromising the essential voluntary nature of the local tidy towns effort, which is its particular strength. This is, indeed, an area of activity in which the concept of "bottom up" initiative was manifest in practice long before the term gained wide currency. The effort and dedication of voluntary local groups in this area deserves particular praise. A central element of the local authority role should be to help promote, encourage and support local initiative and effort. While this approach obtains in very many areas there may be scope for closer co-operation between local authorities and local committees in some instances.

6.16 Particular ways for local authorities to contribute to tidy towns activity might include: assisting in the formulation of longer term strategies by local groups; linking the tidy towns effort more closely with local culture, heritage and history; incorporating relevant social and cultural activities in tidy towns action; providing guidance in relation to aspects such as urban design, landscaping and wild life areas, natural amenities and conservation; action on derelict sites and helping to maximise the contribution of the tidy towns activities to local social and economic revitalisation and development; and generally relating their own work programmes to the overall tidy towns effort.

Litter

6.17 Another area of activity particularly relevant both to the Tidy Towns and to local improvement generally, is litter prevention. In February, 1996, the Minister for the Environment launched a major new anti-litter initiative - *Action Against Litter* - involving local authorities, other public bodies and a wide range of other interests. This initiative, to be sustained over a two-year period, will involve enhanced performance by local authorities generally, including the town authorities. Town authorities can play an important part in promoting the anti-litter initiative, through litter prevention and disposal measures, in street cleaning and refuse collection, through local publicity and by mobilising local support for and input to, measures undertaken in the initiative. The proposals in this report for greater linkage between town authorities and other groups should help to promote the partnership approach required in the action against litter.

6.18   Town authorities other than town commissioners currently have power to employ litter wardens and to take measures to prevent and dispose of litter. The Commission recommends that these functions, which are of obvious relevance to the local authority anti-litter role discussed above, should be retained and insofar as proposals to that effect may emerge in the context of the anti-litter initiative, enhanced and made available to town authorities generally, including former town commissioners.

6.19   Other environmental services or activities capable of specific local delivery should, where possible, be undertaken by all town authorities having the necessary capacity. Environmental activities (in addition to anti-litter measures already referred to) which can be undertaken by town authorities would include: environmental information and awareness initiatives, promotion of recycling and other local environmental objectives. Such functions are relevant to the future role of town authorities in the development and improvement of their towns and could also be incorporated in the proposed town improvement programme.

Chapter 7

Civic and Community Leadership

A prerequisite to the role envisaged for town local government in the future is that town authorities take a strong position of civic leadership. Recommendations for enhancement of this civic role and for increased involvement in social and community matters, are set out in this chapter.

Civic tradition and community leadership

7.1 A characteristic of town local government which was emphasised in various submissions made to the Commission, particularly by local authority members, is its strong civic tradition and closeness to the community. These strengths can help town authorities in playing a strong and active leadership role, and in increased involvement in community development and social matters. An essential feature of a democratically elected town authority should be to provide civic leadership and a public focus for the town and its citizens, as is the case in many European countries. The local authority should be an institution which individuals and groups within a town look to for leadership and support. Equally, the elected members of town local authorities can see their strength and authority as deriving primarily from their local mandate rather than viewing their status as the lowest tier in a centrally-focussed political hierarchy. By providing effective civic leadership and promoting local partnerships, town authorities can help to maximise the overall effectiveness of local resources and initiatives. This can help to build a greater sense of local self-sufficiency, self-confidence and empowerment and to counter attitudes of dependency. This can, in turn, help to mobilise voluntary effort by local groups and individuals towards the improvement and development of the town and also help to generate support for the town authority's own activities in promotion of the town, for example, in areas such as tourism or investment.

7.2 The civic role of the town authority can be especially significant to smaller town authorities which may not be in a position to exercise an extensive operational role in their own right. It was pointed out to the Commission that a civic focus is important for purposes such as ceremonial occasions and visits by delegations from abroad (for example, in connection with cultural matters, town twinning, tourism or industrial development). It must be emphasised, however, that although the Commission considers it important to enhance the civic role of town authorities, it does not regard this role alone as a sufficient criterion for the establishment of a new local authority. The latter issue is discussed specifically in Chapter 10 which includes suggestions for places where fully-fledged local authorities would not be appropriate.

Developing civic leadership

7.3 A more positive role in town development, as recommended in Chapter 6, should increase the town authority's standing and leadership in the community. Visible achievements in these areas are likely to prompt further effort and input on the part of local groups and individuals. Recommendations in this report for improved linkage with local groups and for greater emphasis on quality of service to the public, are also likely to help enhance the public profile of the authority. The public's perception of local authorities and their members and the degree of public awareness of and interest in local authority plans and activities is important to their community leadership role. We encountered differing views in this regard. In some cases a high degree of public support for the town authority was claimed. The traditional relatively high percentage poll at town elections would also support the view that town authorities enjoy a high degree of public interest. However, there are also indications of less positive public attitudes. There seemed to be a fairly widespread feeling that there is scope for improvement of the public image of local authorities and their members. The view was also expressed in some cases that elected members should have a wider and more balanced community base.

7.4   The role of the elected members and their approach to the local community is a crucial element of the authority's civic role. By virtue of their democratic mandate the elected members are uniquely positioned to play a leadership role in relation to the local community. This status is further underpinned by the fact that the members have the primary policy-making and general directional role in the local government system and that the major legal and financial decisions are vested in them. The position of the members was reinforced in a number of respects by the Local Government Act, 1991. For example, their policy making role and their function of representing the views of the local community were given statutory recognition; the special role of the local authority chair and the representational role of members is reflected in the new systems of annual allowances; there is statutory provision for all local authorities to confer civic honours and for the holding of receptions or presentations for distinguished persons; there is provision for involvement in town twinning and a requirement for county level authorities to publish annual reports.

7.5   Town authorities need to make conscious and positive use of their civic functions. We recommend the following approaches to enhance the civic status and community-related role of town authorities:

•   In the discharge of their general functional responsibilities, town authorities should seek where possible to promote civic pride and develop the civic identity of the town. Activities of particular relevance in this regard include: involvement in appropriate ceremonial, cultural and community events and assistance to groups organising such activities; engagement of the public and local groups in civic-minded activities; organisation or support of local exhibitions, competitions, etc; naming of streets and localities; provision of good quality town and street signs; town decoration; provision of promotional and informational material relating to the town and facilities, events, etc.; involvement in local archives, local history and heritage-related activities, as well as various development measures referred to in Chapter 6.

•   Involvement in the organisation or support of local recreational activities and events such as festivals, parades, entertainment, youth and sport activities. Such activities can have positive social effects, without demanding large expenditure and can help to promote a sense of community and civic identity, as well as being recreational outlets, particularly for younger age groups.

- The title Mayor should be applicable to the chair of all town authorities, but individual authorities could have discretion to use the alternative title of Cathaoirleach. The decision should rest with the elected members. The title Mayor seems to be a generally accepted and internationally recognised title for the chairperson of a municipal authority and judging by comments in many submissions to the Commission, is seen as helping to enhance the civic status of the town authority and its chairperson.

- Town authorities can engender increased community support by promoting public awareness of their plans and activities. Practical measures might include: publication of an annual report (or possibly an information leaflet in the case of smaller authorities - every household in a town should receive such a communication annually); issuing of periodic newsletters; holding of an annual (or more frequent if desired) public information meeting/"open day"; liaison with schools with a view to promoting increased awareness of local government. Such initiatives are already being pursued by some authorities. With regard to annual reports or similar publications, the emphasis should not be solely on formal aspects such as financial statements (which are, of course necessary for public accountability) or legal procedures but also on matters such as proposed developments and projects in the town, services to the public (and access to them) and other information of public interest.

- A positive image of local authorities and their members needs to be projected. There may, at present, be an excessive focus in the public mind on the regulatory and revenue-collection functions of local authorities, and a perception that they are not sufficiently dynamic or responsive to community needs. While local authorities might point to functional and financial constraints (which are broader issues, largely outside the scope of this review of town local government), there is scope for promoting greater awareness of the positive achievements of local authorities in the context of the improvements in public information and communication recommended above. Reorientation of the role of town authorities, as recommended in this report, should also help in developing a more positive perception.

- In our consultations with local authority members a need to improve the public perception of the elected members was acknowledged. Concern was expressed about aspects of reporting of council meetings such as undue coverage of debate on relatively trivial or tangential matters. Greater focus on the positive achievements of local authorities should help to redress the balance in this regard. Best practice in the conduct of council business should be promoted. The national representative organisations of local authority members might consider the production of relevant guidelines, or code of practice for meetings which would complement the modernisation of the statutory code currently underway.

- Utilisation by elected members of the full extent of powers available to them, particularly in relation to the broad policy and financial aspects of local affairs, should be promoted. This may involve less preoccupation with day-to-day matters, which are more the province of management, and greater focus on the authority's broader and longer term strategic interests.

This, again, is an area in which the members' associations could play an increased role by, for example, providing information and guidance. The local authority associations can play an important role in promoting best practice and providing support for elected members generally, to assist them in developing and fulfilling their role. Measures to enhance the resources and status of these associations have been taken and proposals by the Department of the Environment for an improved system of two-way dialogue with them in the ongoing development of the local government system, should facilitate this role. Courses or programmes to provide information/training support, particularly for newly elected members, would be an important way of helping to enhance their effectiveness. These should cover, not only legal aspects, but also practical matters relating to the conduct of council business and the wider roles proposed in this report.

- Membership of town authorities should be as broadly based and representative as possible (for example in terms of gender, age groups, areas, sectors, social and occupational groups and relevant local interests), especially in the context of the civic and community-focused roles recommended in this report. This issue is not amenable to specific recommendations by the Commission, other than to suggest that the matter might be given greater attention by the political parties, for example in the selection of candidates. If recommendations aimed at enhancing both the effectiveness of town local government and its public perception have the desired effect, this should, in turn, motivate a wider cross-section of the community to participate in local authority membership.

- In contrast to the position at central government level, the public do not generally tend to identify local authority members closely with the direction of local authority affairs. This may be related to the need, already referred to, for a more active role by members in relation policy and strategic matters. There is, in any event, need for more active and visible performance by the elected members in the leadership and overall direction of the local authority. It is in the interests of a healthy and productive democratic local government system that the elected members are seen to be associated with the successes of the local authority as well as accountable for any deficiencies. This issue also raises possible questions regarding the nature of the local government system as a whole which are outside the scope of this review.

The community and social dimension

7.6 Town authorities can play an increased role in community and social development particularly with the benefit of enhanced civic leadership, as proposed, in co-operation with relevant statutory and other agencies. Many social issues tend to emerge most sharply in urban areas as, in many cases, do positive responses such as the building of community structures and initiatives. Particular local authority functions have a direct or indirect social content, notably in the housing area. Given the importance of social issues in towns and the enhanced community leadership role proposed for them in this report, it is appropriate that town authorities should have a clearer general mandate in relation to the social well-being and development of their areas. It is not intended that local authorities would usurp or cut across the role of specialist agencies in this field - statutory or voluntary - who perform excellent work. However, even smaller town authorities can make a useful contribution in ways which do not demand significant investment of resources, particularly through their statutory function of representing the interests of the local community, through liaison with local community interests and by providing input to the relevant agencies.

7.7 Local authorities are well positioned to help advance community and social development in their areas. Their strengths in this regard include the multifunctional rather than sectoral nature of their role, the fact that many of their functional responsibilities have a significant social impact and in particular, the fact that they, uniquely, hold a democratic electoral mandate to act on behalf of all sections of the local community. This broad mandate was given further specific statutory amplification in the provisions of the Local Government Act, 1991, referred to at 7.4 as well as a general competence to take action in the interests of the local community. The latter power includes social, community and general development. Town authorities have particular advantages. Their proximity to the local community means that they are well positioned to identify local problems, needs and priorities. At a time of increasing urbanisation, changes in traditional community cohesiveness and the emergence of new needs in relation to particular sections of the community (such as the elderly, youth and long-term unemployed), it is desirable that town authorities, with the particular strengths outlined, play a positive role in helping, in conjunction with other relevant interests, to address social issues within local communities. We do not propose to make definitive recommendations as to specific local authority initiatives. This can best be worked out at local level between local authorities and relevant groups and agencies.

Increased social involvement by local authorities

7.8 Historically, the social role of local authorities has consisted mainly in the provision of what might broadly be termed social infrastructure. For example, provision of facilities to secure proper sanitation and public health was a major factor in the development of local government from the mid-nineteenth century onwards. Apart from regulatory functions in the public health and safety areas, the primary emphasis in local authority programmes was, traditionally, on the provision of physical facilities such as water and sewerage networks, waste disposal facilities, public parks and various other amenities. This emphasis was also a past feature of the local authority housing programme - the most significant focus of local authority social responsibility. There has, in recent years, been a major shift in emphasis in housing from a largely building-oriented approach towards a more comprehensive response to housing needs. This is based on a combination of an expanded local authority housing programme and improvements to the existing housing stock, together with the provision of a wide range of options to address social housing needs (as outlined in the policy document *Social Housing - The Way Ahead*, published in May, 1995). Moreover, within the specific area of local authority housing, there is now a greatly increased emphasis on a broader estate management approach with tenant involvement, encompassing a more comprehensive response to the social needs of communities. Clearly, housing will continue to be the most important direct social function of local authorities. The approach now being taken in relation to social housing can serve as a platform for the development of a broader general social role for town authorities in respect of their communities.

7.9 The development role of town authorities, as discussed in Chapter 6, has important social dimensions arising from effects such as potential economic spin-offs, the benefits of public amenities and facilities to the social life of local communities and, in a more general way, by helping to build positive attitudes and confidence locally. A further significant area of involvement by local authorities in supporting community development, is their role as major sponsors of FAS-funded Community Employment projects in the environmental, amenity, arts, heritage and tourism areas. As part of the Local Urban and Rural Development Operational Programme, local authorities are encouraged to build on their current input to community employment by inclusion of opportunities for training and employment of long-term unemployed persons in the action plans to be implemented in each area under the urban renewal sub-programme.

7.10 In recent years many local authorities have built a wide range of activities around their library service. Libraries are a valuable community resource and are among the most positive points of contact between the public and the local authority. They should continue to be an important community and civic focus. Town authorities are not library authorities but increased input by them to library services is recommended at Chapter 8. Library-based activities often extend from their core information-based services, to activities in the area of arts and culture and further to more purely social and community outreach activities. While this is, no doubt, indicative of the diversity of modern library-based services and the use of libraries as public access points, it may also reflect the need for a more general framework for social action by local authorities, including town authorities.

Scope for further social and community involvement

7.11 The scope for greater involvement of town authorities in action targeted at the needs of particular social groups, such as the increasing elderly population and the often socially-vulnerable youth population, should be fully explored. The provision of physical amenities is important in this regard but there may also be scope for more service-oriented approaches. This might include involvement in practical measures, ranging from support for local groups providing services to the elderly, to activities directed towards youth in areas such as sport, recreation and community involvement. Town authorities might also help to promote awareness of and access to services of relevant agencies and to various facilities and amenities operated by local institutions such as sporting bodies, clubs and schools, thereby helping to maximise utilisation of such resources to the benefit of all sections of the local community.

7.12 In some instances, a proactive approach by town authorities may be warranted to help in community capacity-building. It may be possible for the local authority to help build greater social cohesiveness, community identity and self-help, particularly in areas of new urban development or where community identity may be weak or voluntary community structures lacking. Positive action, such as helping to establish appropriate community structures or to implement arrangements like neighbourhood watch or community alert schemes, or assisting the organising of youth-related activities or assistance for the elderly, may be appropriate in such cases. The community/social role proposed for town authorities in this chapter should have a positive effect in relation to community safety and order generally. The town authority's role would, primarily, be that of catalyst or initiator, helping towards the creation of self-sustaining local structures. The power to make bye-laws in the interests of the common good of the local community under the Local Government Act, 1994, may also be relevant in addressing certain social issues locally in some instances.

7.13 A key aspect of town authority involvement in social and community matters is linkage both with local groups and relevant social agencies - statutory or voluntary. Indeed this role may generally be more relevant for town authorities than direct participation in activities or services. Town authorities are strategically placed to help maximise co-ordination between various local bodies in order to help identify possible gaps in services locally and to provide onward input to relevant agencies (for example, in the areas of health, police, education and training, social welfare and local development) regarding local problems, needs and priorities. Local authorities should not act to duplicate the role of other agencies. They should, rather, complement them and help to maximise their effectiveness. They can provide a channel for local input, helping to provide linkage between local community groups and specialist agencies and helping to focus the relevant support services in relation to local social and community issues.

7.14 We are not, accordingly, proposing increased social expenditure by local authorities. That would be a matter for consideration in the context of the relevant services and is not within our terms of reference. We believe, however, that the role proposed for town authorities will help to maximise the effectiveness of the programmes of the relevant agencies (including local authorities) by providing increased input to planning, co-ordination and targeting of efforts. Various matters referred to are already a feature of many local authorities' activities. We believe, however, that there is a need to draw together the different strands and to provide a more explicit and well-defined mandate in the context of a more positive community leadership role for town authorities. This might take the form of a legal provision giving more express recognition to the role of local authorities in promoting social and community development.

Devolution

7.15 The role of town authorities in relation to community and social matters has been considered largely in the context of the existing areas of local authority responsibility, which is somewhat narrower than in most other European states. If the review by the Devolution Commission were to result in greater local authority involvement in such sectors as education, health, policing, local development or social welfare, this would increase the potential social role of town authorities. Even if direct town authority involvement in the provision of some of these services does not come about, the scope for increased linkage with the relevant agencies should be explored. This is particularly relevant in relation to the various local development agencies established in recent years whose activities can have a significant social and community impact.

The civic and community role in perspective

7.16 The role outlined in this and the preceding chapter is intended to address principles and issues raised in Chapter 5 which suggested the need to chart new directions for town authorities beyond traditional areas.   Town authorities can become a focus for town and community development in the broadest sense and develop a lead role which is in tune with modern needs, relevant to the community and readily adaptable to a changing society.   Just as town local authorities owed their origins in the nineteenth century largely to the need to address the urgent social and health problems in towns at that time, there is now reason to believe that a significant element of their future role lies in helping to address the social issues of urban life into the twenty-first century and to advance the social development of their communities.   This role demands a willingness on the part of local authority staff and elected members to adopt new approaches.   In particular, they must be willing to work in partnership with local communities and other relevant agencies and be receptive to new modes of participation.   Various recommendations in this report should facilitate the development of this role, particularly those in Part 4 dealing with ways of improving linkage between town authorities and county councils and local groups.   Ultimately, however, success depends primarily on the conviction and commitment of local authority members and staff.

Chapter 8

Infrastructural, Regulatory and Related Functions

This chapter considers the appropriate role for town authorities as regards the more traditional functions - housing, roads, water, waste, planning and other miscellaneous matters. Section (A) deals with general issues and principles. Section (B) contains analysis and recommendations on specific functional areas.

Section (A) - General Issues

Introduction

8.1 Chapters 6 and 7 chart new directions for town local authorities which will enable them to intensify action in various development areas and to develop new roles in areas where they are particularly well placed to support, stimulate and lead in community, social and general town development. They will, in effect, be able to concentrate on those aspects of town and community development for which they have particular suitability. Chapter 5 referred to certain inherent weaknesses in the present structural system as regards particular services which rest at both town and county level with attendant resource, organisational and operational fragmentation. Mindful of these, this chapter considers the more traditional functional areas and the measures necessary to address such difficulties, and outlines a more appropriate role for town local authorities.

Issues affecting the allocation of functions

8.2 Determination of the appropriate range of functions for town authorities is a central element of this review and one which has a significant bearing on other aspects. Accordingly, the Commission devoted considerable attention to this question, including detailed consideration of town authority functions on an individual function by function basis. As well as considering matters raised in submissions, the Commission had particular regard to recent developments related to the various services and the allocation of functions (including recent legislation) and to data on town authority activities compiled on the basis of returns from individual local authorities showing the current actual position regarding the discharge of functions by particular town authorities. An abbreviated summary of this is given at Appendix 6.

8.3 While we have recommended significant new roles for town authorities in Chapters 5 to 7, the Commission's specific remit did not extend to consideration of the possibility of transferring functions currently vested in other agencies to local authorities, although noting that the outcome of the Devolution Commission's review might well have a bearing on the functional remit of local authorities. In this regard the involvement of town authorities in relevant activities beyond their traditional functional areas would facilitate the future orientation of the role of town local government in accordance with the principles put forward in 5.4 and 5.5. Within these parameters the main issue to be determined is whether a particular function should be discharged at town or county level and whether a particular function is capable of being discharged by all town authorities or only a limited number. We consider that this issue could appropriately be determined in accordance with the principle of subsidiarity whereby each function should be discharged at the lowest practicable level at which it can be discharged efficiently and effectively. In applying this principle, regard must be had to the criteria in the Commission's statutory terms of reference. In particular, proposals for change in the allocation of functions must not result in unacceptable diminution of the effectiveness of local government but rather, if possible, lead to improvement in performance and cost-effectiveness of services.

8.4 We gave particular attention to the need to maximise the potential of town authorities and in particular, to define an appropriate future role for those in the existing town commissioner category whose functional remit is currently very limited. The Commission noted that economies or efficiencies of organisation and scale are a significant and inevitable feature of certain functions, but also that in other cases worthwhile and meaningful functions are feasible for smaller units. The Commission also bore in mind that its terms of reference obliged it to take account of the effectiveness of the local government system as a whole rather than being guided solely by factors relating to specific areas in isolation. While in some instances the organisation of a particular service in the context of a specific centre of population may appear economical; viewed in the context of the local government system as a whole this may not be a valid conclusion. An exclusively narrow focus is also undesirable on equity grounds where there are variations between the revenue bases of different areas. A key determinant therefore, in deciding the allocation of functions to the respective levels of town and county must be the capacity of the former to discharge responsibilities effectively and efficiently within the overall context of local government within the county. This in turn depends significantly on the existing operational scale of particular authorities, their potential revenue base and the implications for local government services in the county as a whole of decisions relating to the allocation of functions.

8.5 A salient feature emerging from the data on town authority activities mentioned at 8.2 is that there is, in the case of a number of local authority functions, a significant difference between the legal or nominal allocation of functions and the current actual position on the ground with regard to the exercise of these functions. For example, many functions which are legally vested in town local authorities are now carried out on their behalf by the county council through formal inter-authority agreements or other more informal local arrangements. Moreover, there are other functions which, while nominally carried out by town authorities, are so discharged largely through use of county council staff or other resources. One conclusion which might logically be drawn from this state of affairs would be that the legal allocation of functions should be brought into line with the factual situation. This indeed is what has tended to occur in recent legislation in areas such as roads and housing which took account of the de facto position in the allocation of responsibilities. The Commission has taken this into account while also giving due weight to the nature of particular functions and the future role of town authorities as envisaged in this report.

8.6 We also consider, however, that weight must be given to the strong feeling on the part of town authorities regarding their particular characteristics and strengths such as civic tradition, community identity and the need to build on these strengths in areas such as local development and community action. The view was expressed by several town authorities that achievements in their towns are attributable very significantly to the involvement of the town authority. Above all, we consider it important to pay particular attention to the role and potential role of the elected members of the town authorities in community leadership. We gave particular weight in favour of recommending a role for town authorities in functions where the representational or policy-making role of the members is significant (as distinct from the purely operational aspect of local authorities which is more the function of management).

8.7 There needs to be a flexible system for determining the allocation of functions so that the most effective arrangements can be arrived at in each case based on local circumstances and maximising the potential for co-operation. The variations in operational arrangements indicated by the data which is summarised in Appendix 6, demonstrate the need for a framework which will allow appropriate adjustments to the basic standard allocation of functions where necessary. Section 59 of the Local Government Act, 1955, provides a general legal mechanism for inter-authority agreements for one local authority to perform functions on behalf of another. Many such agreements exist but we understand that there may be a degree of reluctance to utilise this formal procedure in some instances. Consideration should, therefore, be given to possible improvements in this provision. It would also be useful to supplement it by the extension to all functional areas of certain provisions which currently apply in specific legal codes. For example, the Roads Act, 1993 and the Fire Services Act, 1981, provide for the joint discharge of functions by road and fire authorities respectively. The former also allows for necessary flexibility in associated financial arrangements. Such provisions might usefully be extended to other functional areas. The Housing (Miscellaneous Provisions) Act, 1992 provides a specific statutory mechanism for the transfer of the functions of a housing authority to another local authority. This procedure has been used to confer specific additional housing responsibilities on certain town local authorities in relation to new specialised social housing schemes which generally operate at county level. A similar mechanism might also be appropriate in other functional areas as a means of allowing town authorities to take on additional functions where they have the capacity to do so and where this would make for overall efficiency. Such a procedure would involve a combination of local initiative/agreement and a mechanism for statutory confirmation.

8.8 In the light of the foregoing, our recommendations in relation to the traditional mainstream functional areas are set hereunder. The recommendations in this chapter must be seen in the context of our recommendations generally and in particular:

- those contained in Chapter 12 relating to new organisational and staffing arrangements and improved linkage for town and county members. This is essential to the future functioning of local government as envisaged in this report;

- those in Chapters 5 to 7, inclusive, regarding areas of new or increased town authority involvement and in Chapter 13 regarding their role in improving public access to services;

- those in 8.7 relating to flexibility in local functional arrangements.

Section (B) - Recommendations for Specific Functional Areas

Housing

The current position

8.9 Most State housing services are provided through democratically elected local authorities. The authorities periodically assess housing needs in their areas, provide accommodation and allocate it on the basis of needs, maintain and manage their rented housing stock, operate a range of housing loans and grants schemes and discharge certain regulatory functions in relation to the private rented sector (including standards and registration of properties). Housing policy was most recently set out in *Social Housing - The Way Ahead* published in 1995. The policy document *A Government of Renewal* contained a commitment "that all forms of social housing assistance will be administered by the local authority".

Issues relating to housing functions

8.10 The Commission considers that town authorities should retain their existing range of housing functions subject to some organisational improvements. In adopting this approach the Commission is conscious of the fact that the legal definition of housing functions in relation to various classes of local authorities was recently updated and rationalised in the Housing (Miscellaneous Provisions) Act, 1992 and furthermore that there is a flexible procedure under that Act whereby a function not already legally vested in a local authority can be so vested by way of statutory order. That mechanism constitutes a procedure for transfer of functions between local authorities. Town authorities which have the capacity to take on additional functions can obtain the legal authority to so do. Such orders have in fact been made under the 1992 Act.

8.11 Appendix 7 details the number of houses being rented by each local authority at 31 December, 1994. The national total is 95,735, of which town authorities provide 14,827 or 15.5%. Housing is perhaps the most significant social function of local authorities and one in which the elected members have an important decision-making function. The Commission was satisfied that town authorities should continue to exercise functions such as housing maintenance, allocation, estate management and tenant participation.

8.12 We were aware of arguments which would favour a transfer of the housing construction function to county level, but taking all the issues, on balance, we decided not to recommend such a transfer. An indication of the level of construction activity can be obtained from data on authorised house starts. Appendix 8 sets out this information for each local authority in 1996. In practice the county councils play a significant role in assisting many town authorities to carry out such functions through the provision of the necessary technical expertise for planning, design and supervision of the housing construction programme. In such cases, the town authority role is, from an operational viewpoint, effectively confined to the co-ordinating role of the town clerk. However, to transfer legal responsibility for construction to the county while other housing functions which have a significant social dimension (for example, maintenance; estate management; tenant participation; house allocation) remain with the town authority, could give rise to significant anomalies, including issues related to ownership and associated responsibilities as between the respective authorities. Moreover, while many town authorities rely on the county council for the discharge of their housing construction functions, this is not universally the case. Use of private contract is a feasible option for many town authorities (including planning, design and supervision). According to local authority returns, over half of the urban district councils and boroughs operate without county council input. Even where the town authority relies largely on county council resources to carry through its housing programme, the case for transfer of responsibility will be lessened by virtue of greater operational and organisational integration as recommended in this report (see in particular Chapter 12). The fact that the Commission has not been made aware of significant inadequacies or difficulties in the discharge of housing functions is also a factor in favour of retaining the current distribution of functions, which as already stated, were reviewed as recently as 1992 and confirmed as such by the Oireachtas. In recommending the retention of current housing arrangements, the Commission does so within this flexible statutory framework which takes account of the potential for some town authorities to take on enhanced housing functions or to give up functions depending on their capacity.

Future arrangements

8.13   While not recommending any significant shift in the distribution of housing functions, we strongly recommend that co-ordination and co-operation between town and county authorities should receive greater emphasis, with a view both to maximising efficiency and providing the best and most convenient standard of service to the public. The scope for improved co-operation and co-ordination through greater operational integration between town and county authorities was a particularly influential factor in our consideration of housing functions. This matter is referred to generally in Chapter 12, in which we recommend a joint town and county organisational structure. The extent of practical interdependence already noted in relation to housing construction makes this approach both feasible and necessary in the housing area.

8.14   The more integrated approach should also involve: a more county-wide approach to housing allocations, the pursuit of greater efficiency in revenue collection and housing maintenance and optimum usage of county council professional and technical expertise. We also believe there is scope for the town authorities to play an enhanced role in facilitating public access to town/county housing services. The role of the town authorities in providing improved customer service to the public is important for local government services generally. This matter is dealt with further in Chapter 13 in which we suggest the development of joint services centres. These would provide as comprehensive a range of services as possible without being restricted by town/county organisational distinctions which have little meaning to the public and can cause much inconvenience. There will, of course, be some constraints where specialised expertise may be required for more complex issues.

8.15 In accordance with the principles set out at 8.5 and 8.7, the allocation of housing functions as between town and county authorities should be kept under review so as to achieve a reasonable match between local authority capacity and functional responsibility. This has particular relevance to former town commissioners. There is currently a discrepancy between the nominal legal powers of the latter and the position in reality. The legal powers of town commissioners are much more limited than other town authorities, but functions relating to the provision of local authority housing are still legally vested in them. However, only a minority of town commissioners now exercise any functions (for example, the maintenance and letting of a very small and old housing stock). Most have transferred their housing stock to the county council and for many years no town commissioners have carried out housing construction. In the event that a town authority does not have the capacity to support an effective service, alternative arrangements should be made utilising the appropriate mechanisms of the Housing (Miscellaneous Provisions) Act, 1992.

Roads

Current arrangements

8.16 Public roads are classified into three categories:

- **National roads**: the principal long distance inter-urban routes linking the main ports, airports and urban areas. These account for 6% of the total road network but carry approximately 38% of total road traffic. National roads are divided into primary and secondary categories.

- **Regional roads**: the main feeder routes into national roads and the main links between them.

- **Local roads**: the balance of the public road network, including both county roads and urban roads.

8.17 Currently all town authorities other than town commissioners are road authorities, but responsibility for regional and national roads in towns rests with the county council (in conjunction with the National Roads Authority (NRA) in the planning, design and execution of works on national roads). The current allocation of roads functions is set out in the Roads Act, 1993 under which the functions of borough corporations and UDCs in relation to regional roads in their areas were transferred to county councils. The 1993 Act provided that urban authorities can have operational responsibility for national (subject to NRA approval) and regional roads in their areas by way of local agreements. A few of the larger urban authorities perform the county council national road function in their town areas under long-standing local arrangements which have been continued by agreements following the 1993 Act and similarly, a small number of town authorities retained operational responsibility for regional roads. Conversely, a number of UDCs have made agreements transferring operational responsibility for urban roads in their areas to the county council and others discharge their functions in relation to these roads through the assistance of the county council.

8.18 Town authorities other than town commissioners have responsibility for traffic and parking functions generally under the Road Traffic Act, 1994. These include provision of traffic signs; making of bye-laws governing the types of parking controls to apply in their areas (places subject to parking charges, levels of charge, maximum parking periods, conditions applying to parking, etc.); provision of car parks and making of bye-laws to control them. Since September 1995, local authorities other than town commissioners have responsibility for licensing of taxis and hackneys. Local authority returns indicate that in a small number of cases the traffic functions of UDCs are carried out on their behalf by the county councils under local agreements and in a number of other cases UDCs avail of county council assistance to discharge such functions.

8.19 Town authorities generally, including town commissioners, have power to operate a traffic warden service, to engage in road safety promotion (e.g. mounting local campaigns and employing road safety officers) and to operate school warden crossing services. A small number of town commissioners operate school warden services but none of the other powers mentioned are currently exercised by town commissioners; where such functions are discharged this is done by the county council on behalf of the town commissioners through local agreements. Road safety functions are also carried out by the county councils on behalf of most UDCs. Town authorities (including town commissioners) have a consultative role in the application of local speed limits which are specified in bye-laws made by county councils and county borough corporations. Other roads-related functions such as motor tax, driver licensing and vehicle testing are operated solely at county level.

Issues relating to roads functions

8.20 A practical difficulty raised with the Commission was the existence of dual responsibility for roads functions in an area - the fact that within a town one local authority is usually responsible for national and regional roads while a different authority is responsible for adjacent urban roads. It was strongly represented to us, that the actual operation of the current arrangements in towns, involving separate town and county contact points to the public for different roads in the same town, with different personnel, can be confusing for the public and elected members who may be concerned with small scale matters such as street openings, cleaning, footpath damage, etc. This situation could be resolved by making one local authority responsible for all roads in the town. Some town authorities suggested that they should have such responsibility, but from an operational and economic perspective, there appears to be a greater prima facie case for giving overall legal responsibility to the county councils. The case for this is somewhat stronger than that for transferring housing construction functions, as discussed earlier in this chapter, in view of the following:

- considerations of social and personal service do not apply to the same extent as in housing;

- there are more significant considerations of economies and efficiencies of scale, as retention of separate operational capacity by individual local authorities in a county is unlikely to be maximally cost-effective;

- all roads are physically part of an integral overall network and road usage cannot be segregated into town and county categories;

- the fact that local roads functions of many town authorities are carried out by the county council.

8.21 The Commission gave much consideration to the appropriate allocation of roads functions and on balance decided to recommend against transferring legal responsibility for urban roads to county level, subject to certain conditions set out under. In arriving at this conclusion we were influenced in particular by the following factors:

- In submissions from and meetings with town authorities, roads matters featured as a major concern and priority of the elected members who generally argued for increased powers including certain functions on regional and national roads, ranging from maintenance, street cleaning and public lighting to a total transfer of responsibility. Against this background the Commission feels that to transfer urban roads functions from town authorities to the county council would be perceived as a significant weakening of the role of town authorities and would be likely to have a demoralising effect on the members and officials of such authorities and lessen their public status and credibility.

- While from a technical and operational viewpoint the fact that roads in towns form an integral part of a wider network is a very significant factor, the portion of the network within the town, particularly in town centres, also serves an added role as part of the urban infrastructure and a vital element in the social and economic life of the town. Main streets of towns warrant a level of upkeep different from that in rural or semi-rural areas. They are prominent central thoroughfares for pedestrian and vehicle traffic and usually contain the main commercial and civic focal points of a town. There is likely to be a more immediate and sustained public response to defects in matters such as lighting, damaged kerbs and footpaths, street cleaning, potholes, etc. The extent of litter control is likely to be much greater than rural needs. Town authority members strongly expressed the desire to be able to ensure as far as possible that such considerations are reflected in the exercise of roads functions in towns.

- The likelihood of difficulties arising from having separate road authorities can be greatly lessened by the introduction of more co-ordinated, integrated local operational arrangements between town and county authorities. This approach is referred to further in this chapter and as a general principle in Chapter 12. The joint town/county organisational structure recommended in Chapter 12 should help to ensure that possible diseconomies or loss of effectiveness which could arise from the existence of separate local authorities, are overcome.

- The Commission considers that where serious difficulties arise from the existence of separate road authorities in a town or where a town authority lacks the capacity to support adequately its roads responsibilities, these problems can be addressed through the comprehensive framework set out in the Roads Act, 1993 in relation to inter-authority agreements, financial responsibilities and joint arrangements.

- The fact that roads legislation was recently the subject of a comprehensive review and that the Oireachtas saw fit as recently as 1993 to allow town authorities to retain their roads functions was a very strong factor in influencing the Commission to adopt this approach.

Future arrangements

8.22 The Commission wishes to emphasise that its recommendation for retention of town authority roads functions is strictly contingent on the following important conditions:

- The road system in a town needs to be seen as a totality, irrespective of which authority is legally responsible. This must be accepted by all concerned, especially in dealings with the public and be an intrinsic part of the organisational culture of town and county. There must accordingly be a high degree of operational co-ordination and integration between town and county authorities in the discharge of roads functions, including the establishment of the proposed joint organisational structures and greater co-ordination between elected members.

- The town improvement programme proposed in Chapter 6 should include a specific roads-related element covering roads in the town for which the town authority is responsible, together with those in the charge of the county council. The improvement programme would reflect proposals in the road works programmes of both authorities. However, it would also include proposals on matters arising from broader objectives related to town improvement, amenity or environmental objectives which require special local input and funding beyond what the requirements of road maintenance per se might normally involve. These could include matters such as public lighting, footpath improvements, street furniture, signage, minor traffic management works or safety measures and general amenity/environmental works on town streets. The inclusion of roads-related matters in the town improvement programme would not in any way affect local authority responsibilities under programmes funded by the NRA, Department of the Environment, EU or any other body. It would, however, allow for the town authority to be kept abreast of all roads matters affecting the town.

- The roads-related element of the town improvement programme should be fully co-ordinated and compatible with the county council's overall programme. This is an essential requirement to ensure that the resources of both authorities are combined and operated in an integrated manner to achieve the maximum benefit from public funds. We are particularly aware in this regard of the major emphasis on value for money and effectiveness now being brought to bear on county council road maintenance and improvement programmes.

- The allocation of responsibility for urban roads should be kept under review. Where this review reveals significant inadequacies in the present system, or potential improvements through alternative arrangements, the necessary changes should be made using the provisions in the Roads Act, 1993 or any new general provision as recommended at 8.7. As in the case of housing, however, it is envisaged that the joint organisational arrangements recommended at Chapter 12 should lessen the likelihood of difficulties at operational level.

National and regional roads in towns

8.23   The case put forward by some town authorities for more general legal responsibility in respect of national or regional roads in towns is not accepted. There are very compelling reasons for this. The overall network considerations are far more significant in the case of national and regional roads than in the case of urban roads. The fragmentation which would be involved in giving responsibility to town authorities for the very limited proportion of that network which lies within town boundaries would be totally unacceptable. Indeed it should be noted that the mileage of national roads within towns is progressively decreasing with the continuing development of town by-passes under the national road development programme. The fact that, according to returns from local authorities even the urban roads in almost one third of urban districts are currently dealt with by the county councils is a further reason for not altering the general position regarding responsibility for national or regional roads.

8.24   Where in particular local circumstances an urban authority may possess the necessary capability, it may assume responsibility for regional or national roads in the town. A small number of urban authorities do in fact operate accordingly, reflecting long standing local arrangements. Nonetheless, the reality must be accepted that only some of the largest urban authorities are in such a position and there are strong reasons against any general increase in the number of authorities responsible for the national route network. However, in the interests of a more integrated town-focused approach, street cleaning on all roads in the town should be available for discharge by the town authority. Where a particular town authority would be in a position to carry out effectively any other specific matters relating to non-urban roads in the town local arrangements can be made to allow the town authority to take on a role through the appropriate mechanism (see 8.7).

Former town commissioners

8.25   These authorities are the subject of special recommendations at 9.15 to 9.20. The range of possible functions available to them will include existing traffic and safety matters and street cleaning. While further operational responsibilities in the roads area are not proposed for such authorities generally, the elected members would have an input in relation to matters such as the application of local traffic measures in the town and should be consulted by the county council as regards roads matters affecting the town (through the town improvement programme proposed at Chapter 6) and increased linkage between town and county members proposed at Chapter 12. We also recommend at 9.19 that there should be a mechanism to give town authorities the opportunity to take on specific activities additional to the range of functions generally available to them, subject to capacity and appropriate organisational and financial arrangements.

Water Services

Current position

8.26 Responsibility for providing water and sewerage services is vested in 88 local authorities - 34 county councils and county borough corporations, and 54 borough and urban district councils. Each of the 54 town authorities is a sanitary authority and is legally responsible for the full range of water services. Funding for the construction of water and sewerage schemes is provided through the Public Capital Programme. Where a significant proportion of the capacity of a new scheme is intended to service a particular industrial or commercial development, the local authority is required to seek a capital contribution from the developer towards the provision of the service. There are complex technical and environmental issues associated with water and sewerage projects. The cost of maintaining and operating public water services installations is met by local authorities from their own resources as supplemented by the rate support grant.

Issues relating to water services

8.27 The arguments considered in respect of possible transfer of housing and roads infrastructure to county level apply a fortiori in relation to water services. For example, the spatial scale of water and sewerage schemes now frequently extends well beyond the town area. As in the case of housing and road construction, the functions of many town authorities are either carried out by the county council on their behalf or else they depend on county council assistance to discharge the functions. Another relevant consideration is the fact that water services functions are an important element of overall environmental activities, which generally involve a context well beyond the area of individual towns and in some respects, even of counties.

8.28 An integrated, scientific and comprehensive approach to water resources management is essential. Within such a system, all of the beneficial uses of water can be identified, judgements can be made on how demands can best be met, and measures which are needed to preserve and improve the quality of water resources for all beneficial uses can be determined. The water services programme, which has a dual role in both utilising and protecting water resources, must operate within the wider framework of a comprehensive water resource management strategy. The location and volume of abstractions for water supply purposes and the location of sewage or effluent discharges, as well as the volume and quality of such discharges, must all take account of the overall objective of maintaining the quality of water resources at the highest level required to support various beneficial uses of particular bodies of water.

8.29 County councils and county borough corporations are the primary agencies concerned with the management of water resources for all purposes. The protection of these resources and their rational utilisation for the provision of essential services are critically important aspects of the role of counties and county boroughs. These are responsible for the licensing of industrial and other discharges to waters, with the more complex activities now licensed by the Environmental Protection Agency (EPA). County and county borough councils are also responsible for the preparation of water quality management plans for river catchments, estuaries and other water bodies. Such plans and their implementation often need to be approached on a joint basis by adjacent counties.

Future arrangements

8.30 Having regard to the environmental, technical, spatial, financial and organisational considerations, which point to the need to operate a modern day water resources programme at or beyond county level, it is recommended that responsibility, including associated charges for services, should be transferred to county level. In current circumstances, it is anomalous that urban authorities, many of them with very limited areas and resources, are responsible for public water supply and sewerage arrangements. Indeed it is noteworthy that in many cases the urban authorities, although legally responsible for licensing industrial and other discharges to sewers, have assigned this function to the county councils. The latter already have responsibility under the water pollution code for discharges to waters and have a level of technical expertise in this area. The county councils are also responsible for the fire service which has particular needs for access to adequate water supply points in urban areas. A more effective water resources management system would be achieved through full integration of the sanitary services and water pollution control systems. This should also have advantages for the development of necessary expertise, staff training and more effective general deployment of resources with a fully integrated overall approach to environmental considerations and requirements affecting water resources.

8.31 Another factor relevant to water services is the high cost and level of technical expertise involved with modern treatment plant to achieve compliance with EU requirements. Not only do such facilities involve high capital cost but, more significantly for town authorities with limited resources, their operation and maintenance involves a very significant ongoing level of expenditure which must be met from local resources. It is noteworthy that some town authority members suggested to the Commission that responsibility in this regard should be transferred to county level because of the heavy ongoing burden which such facilities will involve.

8.32 The following more general points apply in relation to the allocation of the water services functions.

- In some cases it may be convenient and efficient for the town authority to carry out certain functions as regards water services. An appropriate mechanism for designation of responsibility (see 8.7) should be available.

- The joint town/county operational structures proposed in Chapter 12 will provide a means whereby matters raised by the public or town authority members can be pursued by the local officials on behalf of the party concerned who should not normally have to take the matter up separately with the county council.

- There needs to be a high level of consultation with town authorities, particularly the elected members, regarding proposals and developments relating to water services and opportunity for them to make input to the county council on matters affecting the town. Recommendations in Chapter 12 relating to co-ordination and interaction between town and county members should help towards addressing this need.

Other Environmental Matters

Waste Management Bill, 1995

8.33 For the future, waste disposal facilities, licensed to high standards by the Environmental Protection Agency, in compliance with EU requirements, will no longer be operationally or financially sustainable at a town level and are quite likely to demand a county or inter-county scale. Under the Waste Management Bill, 1995, which is currently before the Oireachtas, local authority waste management functions will be better regulated and more clearly defined. County and city authorities will be primarily responsible for waste management within their functional areas (including the preparation of comprehensive waste management plans) and will be assigned specific functions and duties in this regard. The Bill, however, recognises the existing role of town authorities and provides an explicit framework for future waste management activities at town level.

8.34 The Bill contains a range of discretionary powers enabling borough corporations and urban district councils to:

- collect waste or arrange with other local authorities or persons for the collection of waste;

- engage or participate in waste recovery activities;

- provide and operate waste facilities (other than for waste disposal), including civic waste facilities at which waste may be deposited by members of the public; and

- continue to operate existing waste disposal facilities (pending their replacement).

8.35 There is provision for the transfer of responsibility for waste management functions from county level to town authorities, where the latter could more effectively perform the function, and for specific functions to be conferred on town authorities for the purpose of facilitating waste prevention, minimisation and recovery. The only limitation on the existing activities of town authorities is that they will not be empowered to establish new waste disposal facilities. This is a recognition of operational realities. Overall, the Bill's provisions will give town authorities the discretion to maximise their potential in the area of waste management, in the light of local circumstances and local authority capacity.

8.36 Town authorities should concentrate on making a maximum input to activities which are particularly significant to the enhancement of the town or which would benefit particularly from the authority's involvement with the local community. In this regard there would appear to be particular scope for town authorities to play an important promotional role in facilitating waste prevention, minimisation and recovery.

Miscellaneous environmental functions

8.37 Promotion of environmental objectives locally and the provision of various local environmental facilities should form part of the town authority role and recommendations in that regard are made in the context of the development role of town authorities at Chapter 6. However, as already observed in the context of water and waste disposal functions, many environmental matters involve a context well beyond the area of individual towns and in some respects even beyond county areas. They also require a scale of technical and economic resources beyond the capacity of town authorities.   These factors are reflected in the existing assignment of the major environmental control functions to county level and more recently to the EPA at national level. In the interests of consistency with the allocation of environmental control functions generally, any remaining regulatory functions in the area of environmental control (e.g. licensing of certain emissions) should be consolidated at county level. This is consistent with the recommendation regarding water services and reflects the general operational situation in practice.

Planning and Development

Current position

8.38 Borough corporations and urban district councils are planning authorities under the Local Government (Planning and Development) Acts, 1963-1993, with the same range of functions as county councils and county borough corporations, including:

-       facilitating development, and protection and improvement of amenities;

-       making and reviewing the development plan; a review is required every five years with any necessary variations or a new plan made;

-       considering and deciding on planning applications, maintenance of the planning register and availability of information;

-       enforcement of planning control, payment of compensation where it arises under the Planning Acts and miscellaneous functions, such as making of special amenity area orders and licensing of roadside facilities;

-       a range of powers related to promoting the development of their areas as set out in Chapter 6 in the context of the development role of town authorities.

8.39 Recent noteworthy trends in the planning and development area include functions in connection with urban renewal schemes, greater concentration on expediting planning applications so as not to

prejudice economic activity and employment opportunities; environmental impact assessment and the extension of the planning system to development by state authorities. These have generally tended to increase the demands on planning services. In the wider socio-economic and cultural context, there has been a growing awareness of the significance of physical heritage.

8.40 The total number of planning applications received by town authorities in 1995 was in the region of 4,300 or about 12% of the number received by county councils. The ability of town authorities to perform their planning functions reflects their size and capacity. Most authorities avail of the services of the technical and professional staff of the county council for development control duties. For development plan preparation, consultants are sometimes utilised. This situation and the trends in the planning service referred to above, raise a question as to the capacity of smaller town authorities to function, on their own, as planning authorities. However, we see the joint operational structure proposed at Chapter 12 as helping to lessen difficulties in this regard.

Future arrangements

8.41 The Commission sees the role of public participation, both in making the development plan and in development control, as critical. This includes both the duties discharged by elected members at town level and involvement by individual members of the public in the development plan process and individual planning decisions. There is a clear need to retain adequate mechanisms and structures for the maintenance of meaningful local involvement in the planning process. We are satisfied that the functions vested in the elected members should continue to be so vested; particularly those concerning the development plan. This is a key factor not only in relation to the physical development of the town, but also the social, economic and general development of the town and the community. It is of fundamental concern to the elected council.

8.42 Town commissioners are not planning authorities and do not have specific functions under the Planning Acts. Separate development plans are made for these towns by the county council as the planning authority. Town commissioners are, however, among the bodies which must be consulted in the development plan-making process and copies of draft development plans for their areas must be supplied to town commissioners for comment. We did consider whether more fundamental change as regards the responsibility for the development plan for such towns should be made. There are difficulties in separating the different elements of the planning function - e.g. the development plan function and the function of development control, which in effect are two sides of the one coin. More importantly the plan-making function is inextricably linked to the role of the county council as the major infrastructural provider.

8.43 For the foregoing reasons it would not be practicable for former town commissioners to become planning authorities at this point. The Commission considered what practical changes might be implemented in the short term to afford greater recognition in the planning process to such town councils. In addition to the existing formal consultative role, the elected members need to be actively involved in the preparation of the development plan. Their views on the review of the plan should as a matter of course be sought at an early stage in the review process and they should be briefed on the basis and implications of proposed provisions of the plan. The elected members should be informed of major development proposals relating to the town and lists of planning applications affecting it should be made available. Provisions under the Local Government (Planning and Development) Regulations, 1994 in respect of specified development by or on behalf of local authorities, require them to send notice of the proposed development to any local authority whose area appears to be affected. All town councils should be notified under this provision. This would provide them with an opportunity to make submissions on developments proposed by the county council in the town. The more integrated organisational arrangements together with improved linkage for town/county elected members, recommended elsewhere, should greatly improve the position for such town councils in the planning area. In the longer term the possibility of further statutory recognition or of an increased role for such town councils should be explored in the context of the review of planning law.

8.44 An entirely separate issue is the question of co-ordination between the statutory development plans of the town planning authorities and the county councils. In some cases, the legal town boundary is a source of difficulty in planning terms. The main concentration of development often tends to be in town environs, outside the administrative town boundaries. There has been an increasing need to draw up parallel development plans for the environs as well as for the town itself. In some cases, plans are prepared jointly by the town and county authority for the entire town area. However, in other instances the town authority and the county council draw up separate plans for the town and environs - often at different times - which may not fully dovetail in all respects. It is clearly undesirable that this position may obtain in respect of what, for planning purposes and in the eyes of the public, constitutes a single urban settlement.

8.45 Where growth has extended beyond old legal boundaries, different authorities under different planning pressures may seek to pursue different objectives. This may be especially marked in the cases of towns divided by county boundaries. While boundaries are necessary for electoral and administrative purposes, the planning and consequential financial implications can be significant. Apart from any issues of boundary revision, it will still be desirable to have improved co-ordination in the making of development plans. There should be a single plan, prepared jointly covering the town and its environs (including cross-county environs) to be adopted by both the town and county authorities concerned, each in relation to the area within its jurisdiction covered by the plan. For ease of use, and understanding, this should be produced as a single document. We recommend all future reviews of town development plans should be carried out jointly and the plan prepared on this basis as a single document covering the entire town.

Library Services

8.46 The importance of the local authority library service as a public amenity and a community resource is referred to at 7.10. Responsibility for local library services now rests with the county level authorities. This has come about through a process of local transfer of library powers by town authorities over many years. In view of this, and the advantages of a unified service (e.g. for book circulation) no transfer of library responsibility to town authorities is proposed. However, we do feel that there is scope for greater involvement by the elected members of town authorities in the development of local library services. Town authority members should have a formal right of consultation and input in relation to statutory library development programmes under section 33 of the Local Government Act, 1994 and we recommend accordingly. We also recommend that where there are county library committees or joint committees, town authority members should have representation on them as is already the case in many counties. In counties containing several town authorities a process would need to be devised (such as rotation) to avoid unwieldy committee size. There should also be a framework whereby town authorities could make an input to library development projects either from their own resources or through the organisation of local contributions. The Commission also notes that new powers in the 1994 Act in relation to local records and local archives apply to all town authorities. The relevance of this function and activities in other areas of local history, heritage and culture, to the civic and community-related roles of town authorities are referred to in Chapter 7.

Casual Trading

8.47 Town authorities, other than town commissioners, have various functions in relation to the regulation of casual trading, including the making of bye-laws and designation of casual trading areas under the Casual Trading Act, 1995. In view of the fact that this matter has been the subject of a recent review and subsequent legislation, the Commission does not consider it appropriate to recommend any change other than to suggest that the elected members of town authorities who do not have direct powers (i.e. former town commissioners) should have a right of consultation and input in relation to the making of casual trading bye-laws affecting their town.

Fire and Emergency Services

8.48 Local authorities have various functions relating to public safety including the fire service, civil defence and action in response to emergency situations. These functions are mainly vested in the county level authorities. Only three of the larger urban authorities are fire authorities. Building control functions are organised on the same basis as the fire service and most other emergency response activities are similarly connected to the fire and emergency role. There are compelling practical considerations of co-ordination, logistics, expertise and resources for organisation of the fire and emergency services at county level and indeed beyond that level in the case of elements such as the regional Computer Aided Mobilisation Project which facilitates mobilisation, communications and response arrangements for fire authorities. We accordingly recommend no change in these arrangements. There is, however, a case for integration of the three urban fire authorities with the relevant county fire services where this would provide the most effective arrangement in the light of all the circumstances. In this regard we note that the recent reorganisation of local authorities in Dublin involved the introduction of a unified fire service for the city and three counties.

Derelict Sites

8.49 A matter of relevance to local town improvement functions considered in Chapter 6 is the exercise of powers under the Derelict Sites Act, 1990. Town authorities, other than town commissioners, have powers and duties in relation to measures to prevent and control derelict sites such as: maintenance of a derelict sites register; requiring measures to be taken in relation to derelict sites; acquisition of derelict sites and charging a levy on derelict sites. In the case of town commissioners' areas the functions rest with the county council. No change in this allocation of functions is proposed but the Commission recommends that former town commissioners be given an appropriate involvement and consultative role in relation to policy to deal with the problem of derelict sites. Action in this area could also form part of the town improvement programme.

Burial Grounds

8.50 Town authorities, other than town commissioners, currently have functions relating to the provision and operation of burial grounds. There are arguments for transferring this function to the county councils. This function was originally vested in urban authorities in nineteenth century legislation at a time when their public health and sanitary functions constituted a very significant element of their role. The role of town authorities has now evolved in largely different directions. On the other hand the provision of burial grounds is an important community service and on this account we feel that town authorities should, in principle, retain responsibility with the option of entering into agreements for discharge of functions by the county where they so wish. This is also an area in which voluntary local groups tend to play an important role (e.g. in cleaning and maintenance of burial grounds); local authorities can encourage such involvement.

Administrative Matters

8.51 All local authorities have power to engage in administrative operations such as the provision of office accommodation and equipment, land acquisition and revenue collection. Powers in these areas should remain but there should be adequate co-ordination and integration between town and county authorities with a view to maximising effectiveness, efficient use of resources and quality and convenience of service to the public. For example, decisions relating to office location and use of information technology should take account of factors relevant to enhancing co-ordination between authorities and the provision of a comprehensive and integrated public service. Insofar as office accommodation is concerned, every opportunity should be availed of to arrive at a situation where town and county services are located in the same building or complex. We believe that in the long term, significant savings, increased effectiveness and better public service can be achieved by such an approach. Similarly, in the area of revenue collection, there may be scope for achieving greater efficiency through more integrated arrangements between town and county authorities. There are also likely to be cost and efficiency benefits from central provision of accounting, management information and other similar support services through the use of information technology. The scope for greater cohesiveness and integration generally is dealt with specifically in Chapters 12 and 13.

Part
3

Structural
Arrangements

Chapter 9

Town Classification

This Chapter recommends an appropriate future classification of town authorities

Current classification

9.1   There are currently 114 elected local authorities in five legal classes as follows:

Class of Authority	Numbers
County/City Authorities	
county councils	29
county borough corporations	5
Town Authorities	
borough corporations	5
urban district councils	49
town commissioners	26
TOTAL	**114**

9.2   The framework of town local government grew up through a series of separate statutes, principally in 1840, 1854, 1878 and 1898. Some town authorities even trace origins back to medieval British Royal Charters. In the first decades of independence a small number of individual town authorities were abolished or reclassified. More recently, new town commissioners for Shannon, Greystones and Leixlip were established. The various Acts provided for different types of authorities with varying functions, not always fitting in well with already existing structures. In other words, there has never been a single comprehensively designed system of classification for town authorities. While most European countries have a comprehensive set of sub-national territorial structures, the Irish pattern of entirely separate town authorities is probably unique in the modern era. While the county and city areas, the primary unit of local government, cover the entire state, the towns are isolated units within this tier. By comparison, the basic local authority units in France - the Communes - together cover the area of the entire State, though ranging in population size from under a hundred to over 2 million. In contrast, Irish town authorities are small islands within the county tier, ranging in population size from 459 to 25,843.

Classes of local authority

9.3   For electoral purposes the county is divided into a number of county electoral areas - the councillors' constituencies. The county electoral areas include all towns located within them (including local authority towns) and the combined electoral areas cover the full county. The county council is thus elected by the entire population of the county. Town residents vote in two separate elections, one for the town authority and one for the county council. In general, the county council is legally responsible for all functions in areas outside of those towns which have a separate town local authority (i.e. non local authority towns, villages and rural areas) and for certain functions (e.g. motor tax, library, fire service, etc.) throughout the entire county including all the towns. The county borough corporations - the authorities for the five major cities of Cork, Dublin, Galway, Limerick and Waterford - are of equivalent status to counties. They do not contain separate town authorities and are, accordingly, outside the scope of this review.

9.4 There are currently eighty town authorities in three separate classes, boroughs (5), urban districts (49) and towns with town commissioners (26), located within and forming part of administrative counties. The five boroughs, on the basis of the existing administrative boundaries, have areas ranging from 227 hectares (Wexford) to 1,238 hectares (Drogheda) and populations ranging from 8,515 (Kilkenny) to 23,848 (Drogheda). The forty-nine urban districts, have areas ranging from 67 hectares (Trim) to 2,443 hectares (Dundalk) and populations from 1,463 (Bundoran) to 25,843 (Dundalk). The twenty-six other towns, have areas ranging from 24 hectares (Ballybay) to 1,010 hectares (Bantry) and populations ranging from 459 (Ballybay) to 13,194 (Leixlip). The present classification of towns derives mainly from historical factors and the way in which different Acts affected the structural/functional make up of the local government system. It is difficult to see any logical principles underlying the current arrangements. It should also be noted that the built-up area of many towns extends beyond their administrative boundaries and some towns are divided by county boundaries - see Chapter 11.

9.5 Town commissioners have a very limited range of functions and a consequential low level of expenditure and minimal staff (see Appendix 2). Almost all functions in these towns are the responsibility of the county council. In practice, the role of the commissioners is mostly representational - to provide a democratic voice for the town. Some towns, particularly the more recently established ones, undertake local activities and community support of varying kinds, but to a necessarily limited degree.

9.6 There are seven counties (Dun Laoghaire-Rathdown; Fingal; Laois; Leitrim; Limerick; Roscommon and South Dublin) without boroughs or UDCs and the relevant county council is accordingly responsible for all services throughout the entire county including all towns (except for the very limited matters dealt with by town commissioners in Fingal, Laois and Roscommon).

9.7 Borough corporations and UDCs are equivalent for most practical purposes and have generally the same legal range of functions. However, some boroughs and larger UDCs have more extensive powers in certain areas (e.g. housing, fire and roads; but not necessarily the same authorities in each of these services). Apart from the latter, the main distinguishing factor other than historical background is that boroughs have mayors, while UDCs have cathaoirligh/chairpersons (again a ceremonial rather than practical distinction). Boroughs and UDCs have legal responsibility for planning, housing, water services, local roads, rating, amenity and other miscellaneous functions in their own areas. In practice functions statutorily vested in some urban authorities (especially smaller UDCs) are actually carried out by the county council. However, arrangements vary as between individual authorities and for different services, with in some cases a very substantial county council input, while in others this is limited. There does not appear to be a correlation in all cases between size of authority (as indicated by, for example, population) and the extent to which urban authorities carry out functions themselves or through arrangements with the county council. Appendix 6 gives an overall indication of the position in this regard by way of summary data derived from returns from local authorities.

9.8 There are certain services e.g. fire, and building control; emergency planning; library service; motor tax; national and regional roads, for which the county council is legally responsible in most cases throughout the entire county including the boroughs and urban districts. In the county area outside of boroughs and urban districts, the county council is responsible for all services. The county manager, as well as being the manager of, and an officer of, the county council, is also manager for any boroughs, UDCs and town commissioners within the county.

New classification

9.9 The present situation of three differently styled sub-county authorities is confusing and largely meaningless to the public, especially as these titles all apply to what is in each case a "town". In the context of the renewal of town local government, every effort should be made to project a positive and meaningful image, including the use of meaningful titles. While different town authorities may exercise different functions (as happens in practice at present) there will not, in future, be different types of sub-county authorities - all will be town authorities. We recommend, accordingly, that there should be a single title or classification for all town authorities. The title should be "Town Council" which will be of immediate meaning to people generally. The chairperson of all town councils should be titled Mayor, the internationally recognised term. If, however, individual local authorities wish to use the term "Cathaoirleach" or "Chairperson", this should be a matter for local decision.

9.10 If the existing "borough corporations" wish to continue to use that term as a ceremonial title for reasons of local history, civic status, etc, they could continue to do so but the generic legal title would be "town council". We also recommend that the term "county borough", which is of little or no meaning to the layperson or local government customer, should be dispensed with and replaced by the term "city" and the local authority termed the "city council". This will provide a meaningful and comprehensive set of terminology for local government structures as follows:

Area	Local Authority
City	City Council
Town	Town Council
County	County Council

9.11 At present the functions of town authorities are determined largely by the class of authority. But even here there are significant variations. The fire service is generally a county council function but three authorities (two UDCs and one borough corporation) are, by law, fire authorities and are also building control authorities which is also generally a county function. Recent housing and roads legislation also contains legal provision for transfer of what are generally county functions. The Waste Management Bill currently before the Oireachtas also allows for such arrangements. Apart from these legal provisions, in practice many town functions are actually carried out by or with substantial input from county councils, by way of formal agreements made locally or more informal local arrangements. All of this tends to show that the most meaningful determinant in the allocation of functions is town capability and local arrangements not the fixed legal classification of the authority. It will be noted that in the case of the functions referred to above, their allocation or non-allocation to particular UDCs or borough corporations does not alter that classification. Indeed the responsible authority for a particular service (e.g. the fire authority, housing authority, etc.) is defined in a manner which can accommodate the diverse local circumstances, and the degree of correspondence between functions and classification has tended to reduce over the years, both in law and practice.

9.12 Clearly, therefore, functional allocation does not have to derive from the titles used - that would be a case of "the tail wagging the dog" - and there are good reasons for a single title for all town authorities. The main criteria in assignment of functions should be quality of service, efficiency and value for money of the system as a whole and the capacity and effectiveness of particular authorities to deliver services. The capacity of an authority depends not only on available financial resources but also to a great extent on its existing base of activity. Indeed, population size may be of little relevance in this particular context. The fact that all town authorities in a range of population sizes would come under the same formal title should not cause a problem. The French example, already mentioned, illustrates this, with the term "Commune" covering places of less than 50 population as well as the city of Paris. Indeed this situation applies in several European countries.

9.13 There should be flexibility in the assignment of functions at local level. This should be determined as far as possible on the basis of local circumstances rather than being centrally imposed. The statutory framework should allow arrangements for delivery of functions in towns to be tailored to local circumstances, rather than being straitjacketed solely on the basis of classification. This general approach has been evident in recent legislation referred to above. The single "town council" classification avoids attempting to arbitrarily constrain functional responsibility within a priori classification, as might be the case with a multiple classification system.

9.14 Within the proposed classification, all town councils would have a general representational role and functions in relation to town and community development and improvement as set out in Chapters 6 and 7 and, to the extent recommended in Chapter 8, in the more traditional areas of local authority activity. In short, while there would only be a single class of town authority, there would be a range of functions from the lowest to the highest but this would be a continuum, rather than a series of homogeneous functional sub-categories based on arbitrary criteria, such as population. The system would accommodate diversity and subsidiarity, with arrangements (involving both decisions locally at inter-authority level and appropriate statutory mechanisms for functional allocation) to match functions to authorities' individual circumstances. The town improvement programme proposed in Part 2 will provide an improved framework for activities in the area of development and related matters, including roads. The joint staff and organisational structure proposed in Chapter 12 will facilitate the efficient discharge of functions at operational level. Revised financial arrangements, probably involving a more unified county-wide approach as discussed at Chapter 15, will help to ensure that the respective functional responsibilities of town and county authorities are underpinned by a rational system for determination of financial responsibilities.

Former town commissioners

9.15 It is necessary to make special reference to the position of former town commissioners in the new town classification. The term "town council" would apply equally to such authorities as would the office of Mayor. Their responsibilities would be determined by reference to a range of possible functions which would be available to them, the decision to take on such functions being made by them on the basis of considerations of capacity, overall efficiency and service to the public. In this regard it must be recognised that the future role of these authorities cannot be viewed in isolation from either their current position or their place in the overall county system. Their future development must evolve from that position.

9.16 Town commissioners now have few powers and only minimal financial and organisational resources. It was evident from submissions that some town commissioners see their future role as primarily a civic one, together with the exercise of some local development and promotional functions. We believe that even the smaller authorities can and should exercise an enhanced role in these areas and in representing and promoting the interests of their local communities. Accordingly, all such authorities will have available to them the roles outlined in Chapters 6 and 7 in the areas of development and civic and community-related activities.

These authorities would, therefore, be able to have involvement in relation to such matters as:

- representation of the local community and liaison with local groups and input to relevant public and other agencies, particularly with a view to promoting development and social/ community objectives;

- development of local amenities, town improvement and promotion initiatives (e.g. in relation to local tourism), in conjunction with the county council and possibly other local interests;

- local environmental activities (e.g. environmental improvements, clean-up campaigns and information and awareness initiatives, street cleaning, litter prevention, operation of litter warden services);

- tidy towns activities and related matters such as planting, street furniture and similar town improvements;

- promotional activities, in conjunction with the appropriate national agencies, in areas such as fire, water and road safety (possibly through co-operation with schools or other local bodies);

- naming of streets and localities, provision of nameplates, provision of informational material and other similar initiatives to enhance civic identity;

- civic functions such as town twinning, civic honours, receptions for distinguished persons and other civic or ceremonial occasions;

- input to social, recreational, leisure and cultural activities and events such as festivals, parades, exhibitions, and competitions;

- operation of or input to local archives and promotion of matters related to local heritage and history;

- other initiatives to promote the interest of the local community under the general competence provision of the Local Government Act, 1991.

Where the town authority takes on functional responsibility this brings financial responsibility. In the circumstances of the former town commissioners the most effective arrangement generally is likely to be one of joint responsibility between the town and county authority, with each making an appropriate input. The proposed town improvement programme will provide a suitable framework to determine this and to enable the town authority to exercise a meaningful role in those areas outlined above which require joint input. Where the town authority wishes to advance particular projects in that context, it may be possible to supplement its input and that of the county council through the organisation of ad hoc local financial input as discussed at Chapter 6. Implementation of measures under the town development programme or otherwise in relation to the town will be facilitated by the integrated operational structure proposed in Chapter 12.

9.17 Other ways in which the position of former town commissioners will be enhanced through recommendations in this report include:

- participation in a system of structured consultation with representatives of the county council (e.g. the area committee) as proposed in Chapter 12, which will enable the authorities to play a more effective representational role;
- creation of an office of Mayor which should help to enhance the civic status of the authorities;
- issuing of informational material regarding the authority's activities;
- participation in a formal system of consultation with representatives of local groups, which should serve to strengthen the authorities' community and civic leadership role;
- representation on library committees where appropriate;
- participation in joint services centres (see Chapter 13) in certain towns through an evolutionary process involving expansion of county council area offices.

9.18 Within the areas discussed in Chapter 8 the role of town commissioners is necessarily limited. It is envisaged that town councils which were in that category would continue to have existing powers available to them in relation to such matters as: making of bye-laws under the Local Government Act, 1994; traffic warden services; current housing functions; consultation in relation to speed limits and development plans; road safety promotion and school warden crossings. The availability of these functions and those set out at 9.16 would be on the basis that the necessary operational capacity would, in future, be available through the proposed joint operational structures. However, having regard to the current low level of utilisation of some such powers (notably in the housing area), transfer of responsibility through the mechanisms referred to at 8.7 may be appropriate in some cases. We wish to emphasise, however, that it would not be valid to regard the potential of the former town commissioners primarily from the perspective of the infrastructural and regulatory type roles of the larger authorities. Instead, a significant element of their role will be to mobilise and where possible support, action by local groups and communities to advance the interests of the towns. The role of the elected members is particularly important in this regard.

9.19 The elected members will also be in a position to have significantly increased input to and influence on matters for which the county council is responsible, through participation in the proposed town improvement programme, the system of enhanced interaction between town and county members recommended in Chapter 12 and improved consultation procedures in relation to various functions dealt with in Chapter 8 such as planning, traffic and parking, libraries, casual trading and derelict sites. Consideration might also be given to bringing such authorities within the ambit of certain discretionary functions in the area of waste management such as waste prevention and minimisation activities. There should also be a mechanism to allow former town commissioners to take on specific additional functions available to other town authorities, where they have the resources and capacity to support these and where this would not give rise to inordinate additional cost or loss of effectiveness. This would be conditional on establishment of the integrated operational structures recommended in Chapter 12 and revised financial arrangements as discussed at Chapter 15. The procedure would involve a combination of local initiative/agreement and a mechanism for statutory confirmation. It must, realistically, be recognised that the number of cases in which this procedure is likely to operate would be very limited and, in view of the need to avoid fragmentation of resources and organisation, it is desirable that it should only arise where there is clear justification.

9.20 The question of increased powers and functions for former town commissioners brings into very sharp focus the constraints placed on the Commission by the restrictions of its terms of reference and by the practical realities of existing resources and organisational capacity. The Commission's recommendations are designed to enhance the role of the former town commissioners as far as possible and we believe that the recommendations in preceding paragraphs will allow for this provided the authorities concerned grasp the opportunity. However, the need (as set out in the 1994 Act) to secure maximum benefit from the operation of the local government system generally; for effectiveness, efficiency and economy and best use of resources and to safeguard the position of county councils as the primary units of local government, restrict the scope for widening the areas of separate responsibility of former town commissioners on a general basis. The following factors are particularly significant in this context:

- The extension of separate rating powers to former town commissioners could have seriously adverse effects on the revenue base of the county council, especially in smaller counties or those containing more than one such town. Evidence to this effect was obtained from sample studies carried out on behalf of the Commission.

- In addition to an adverse financial impact on the county council, there would be significant net additional cost to the local government system as a whole if separate administrative establishments (say to the level of the average UDC) were to be created for former town commissioners. This, again was demonstrated in data obtained as part of the sample studies referred to above. Administrative staff and associated overheads required to administer such functions separately for a town authority are not likely to be matched by proportionate savings to the county council, due to indivisibilities and to the loss of scale economies which apply in the county context. It would not be desirable that the creation of administrative organisations for former town commissioners should absorb resources which might otherwise be available for the provision of services. Alternatively, additional cost would fall on taxpayers, ratepayers or service charge payers. Clearly, decisions leading to any such expansion would have to be carefully considered and the implications made clear to the public. We have recommended at 12.17 that any development of the organisational capacity of town commissioners should evolve (to the extent necessary), as part of the proposed joint structures, with joint services centres being developed through expansion of county council area offices, where appropriate.

- Some smaller towns are unlikely to have sufficient revenue base (currently in the form of town charges determined by the commissioners and added to the county rate for the town area) to support the undertaking of any significant increase in the areas of activity of the town authority as a separate entity, which would fall to be met by the town itself. The sample studies showed that if some former town commissioners became separate rating authorities with functions and scale of activity equivalent to an average UDC, the result would be a dramatic increase in rate poundage (even though some of these towns were sizeable in population terms). The reality in such cases at present is that investment in the town is, and will continue to be, heavily dependent on the county council. Moreover, where existing arrangements are operating successfully it is essential that such success is not impaired through, for example, fragmentation of effort between town and county authorities. The town improvement programme and other means of enhanced interaction will give the town authority members a greater influence over decisions in this regard and in relation to county council functions generally in the town area without carrying separate legal/financial responsibility.

9.21 We feel that there is need to give particular attention to the progress of the smaller town councils. In the possible event that some of these do not prove capable of developing successfully along the lines envisaged it may be desirable to consider alternative approaches, possibly in the context of variation in the terms of reference which applied to this review. In the context of a renewed system of town local government in which an appropriate range of meaningful functions would be available to even the smallest town authorities, if it transpires that some authorities are unwilling, or lack the capacity or fail to grasp the opportunity to take on the new roles outlined (at least in the medium term if not immediately), this must call into question the longer term statutory status of such authorities.

Town council status for all towns

9.22 County borough corporations, (which we have suggested should be titled "city councils"), do not, per se, come within the scope of our review. It was suggested to us, however, that the county borough structure might be applied to some towns. County boroughs have equivalent status and powers to county councils and are entirely independent of them with their own city manager and independent organisations. The smallest county borough is bigger than some of the smaller counties. In addition to considerations of scale and viability, it would be wholly inappropriate to consider establishing new county borough structures and thus entirely separating any town concerned from its county. The whole thrust of this report is to achieve a more coordinated and cohesive local service with all the benefits this entails for service to the public, for staff and members and for organisational effectiveness. We must, therefore, reject such suggestions which would lead to further fragmentation of the local government system.

Chapter 10

New Local Structures

This chapter recommends procedures for the possible establishment of local authorities or alternative structures in towns which do not currently have local authority status.

Introduction

10.1   The Commission is required to make proposals in relation to appropriate criteria and procedures for the establishment of a local authority in a town where there is currently no local authority. The 1994 Act does not require the Commission to make recommendations in relation to specific towns, but rather to recommend general criteria and procedures. However, it is relevant to have regard to the size and distribution of existing non-local authority towns. Appendix 9 contains a list of almost one hundred such towns having a population of at least 1,000 or more at the 1991 census.

Submissions

10.2   Submissions to the Commission on the issue of possible new town authorities included views or proposals which fall into four broad categories:

- those seeking the traditional elected local authority with functions on the lines of current UDCs or, in a few cases, a somewhat reduced regulatory/infrastructural role with emphasis mainly on matters such as planning, traffic management, street cleaning, cycle lanes, public lighting, footpaths, amenities, local development and promotion and liaison with outside bodies;

- some form of (unspecified) structure to help secure improved local services and greater focus on town development;

- a mainly ceremonial or representational focus for the town for tourism, town twinning and the like, e.g. some form of officially recognised "community council" with certain enhanced status;

- a view that there is no necessity for the establishment of additional local authorities.

Some submissions favoured the establishment of local authorities in almost all towns; others cautioned against the creation of "mere debating chambers". A possible alternative to the town authority model was also suggested, viz. a wider area body incorporating neighbouring towns.

10.3   The main concern seemed to be a desire for greater focus on development and promotion of the town and a vehicle to achieve improved local services. A perceived need for ceremonial or representational presence in the town (e.g. for town twinning and reception of visitors) and for provision of information about the town seemed to be a motivating factor in other cases. Suggested benefits of establishing a separate town authority included enhanced local identity, a means of generating increased input from local groups and individuals, better linkage with the local community and more convenient public access to local government, the possibility of more effective representation and better input to decision-making and service delivery.

10.4   Submissions contained a wide range of views as to criteria for possible new authorities. Most envisaged a minimum population threshold, varying from as little as 500 to 10,000. Other factors suggested included the existence of established community identity, community demand for a town authority and the need to take account of the effects on the county councils' finances. Views were also expressed that there is no necessity to establish new local authorities.

Recently established authorities

10.5   In the recent past, the demand for new town local authorities has been greatest in the context of towns experiencing rapid expansion, where there is often a perceived need to establish a new identity and structure focused particularly on town needs within the political/administrative system. The only new town authorities established in recent years were Leixlip (1988), Greystones (1984) and Shannon (1980) town commissioners. None of these has a population of less than about 8,000. On the other hand, a number of town commissioners went out of existence in the first half of the century through a variety of circumstances. These included the town commissioners for Callan, Fethard, Newcastle West, Rathkeale, Roscommon and Tullow.

Scope for additional town authorities

10.6   The 1991 census shows almost one hundred towns outside of Dublin with population size over 1,000 which do not have a separate town local authority. At present the smallest local authority town has a population of under 500 within its legal boundaries (or around 1,100 inclusive of environs). It must be remembered that the town local authority system has evolved in a haphazard fashion over many years. Current structures and classification bear no relationship to population size or any other logical principles.   If authorities of the current small size were to be replicated systematically across the country for all similar towns, there is potential for proliferation of additional authorities.

Cost and other relevant factors

10.7   Criteria for the possible establishment of new authorities must take account of likely financial, organisational and strategic implications. Formal elective local authorities - even if only having a purely representational role - involve unavoidable costs. If a new authority is to exercise a significant range of functions, the potential cost is correspondingly high. All additional public authorities bring with them overheads - costs related to staffing, accommodation, members, general administration. Reference is made at 9.20 to findings of a sample study of the likely effects of expanding the functions of existing town commissioners to a scale equivalent to an average UDC. This showed a likelihood of substantial overhead costs, aside from expenditure on provision of services, with similar increases in rates or charges, especially where the revenue base in the town is low. The effect of establishing a new town authority with similar functions is likely to correspond to or exceed this. In the latter case, the organisation has to be built up from scratch and the problems of indivisibilities, loss of scale economies related to overheads, and likely non-correspondence of savings for the county council to costs in the new authority, would be felt even more severely.

10.8 There is also danger that the establishment of new town authorities may cause further fragmentation, duplication and dilution of available resources. There is every likelihood that expenditure on the overheads of the new authority would result either in diversion of resources from services or investment in the town, or else result in corresponding increases in rates or charges. We are particularly mindful in this context of the requirement in our statutory terms of reference to have regard to the need for effectiveness, efficiency and economy. Where existing arrangements in terms of service provision and town development and promotion are operating effectively, there is clearly need for caution as to any changes which might adversely affect such arrangements.

10.9 In addition to considerations such as organisational overheads and diseconomies, fragmentation of decisions relating to services and their financing could be very damaging from an overall strategic and fiscal perspective and in terms of equity. In the event that the town has a substantial revenue base, the consequential effect on the county council is likely to be significant and in the event of there being a number of such towns in a particular county, the cumulative effect would be particularly severe. It is difficult in such circumstances to reconcile proposals for new town authorities with the statutory requirement to safeguard the position of the county council as the primary unit of local government. While a few towns with a high revenue base might support certain local services on a stand-alone basis, possibly even to an above average standard, the proliferation of such isolated decision-making and financing could weaken the viability of the overall local government system and the standard of service which could be provided throughout. Equally, there is a danger that some small authorities, established with an understandable desire to enhance local representation, could prove unsustainable in the long term. We are concerned that the local government system must be founded on units which are rational and sustainable both in fiscal and organisational terms. This is essential if, as appears to be the desire of most elected members, local authorities are to have a significant base of local discretionary funding, as distinct from high dependence on central grants, and if the potential for devolution of functions to local government is to be maximised. These issues are especially relevant in the context of the current finance and devolution reviews.

10.10 The system of local government which we have encountered is affected by problems of fragmentation - structural, organisational and financial. We have sought to address this through recommendations for greater cohesiveness. It is essential that a new element of fragmentation is not introduced by widescale accretion of new small town authorities. We make a conscious distinction between the problems associated with establishing new authorities and retention of many existing small authorities. Existing small urban district councils already have an organisational basis which in future will be enhanced as part of the joint organisational framework recommended in Chapter 12. Recommendations have been made in Chapter 9 for the former town commissioners, taking account of their limited current role and resources. The Commission's terms of reference did not, of course, include an option of rationalising the range of existing town authorities. Aside from that, however, the Commission recognises the achievements of many small authorities and is confident that, through the more integrated arrangements being recommended, they will have the opportunity to make an important contribution.

10.11 We are satisfied that creation of new town authorities on a wide scale - for example, so as to replicate authorities in all towns of the scale of current local authority towns (see 10.6) - is totally unsustainable. The existence, by virtue of historical circumstance, of town authorities in a number of small towns, is not in itself a premise on which to base a case for the creation of new authorities in all or any other towns of that size. It must be remembered that many existing town authorities were established as far back as the mid-nineteenth century when perceptions of scale were far different from now, not only relative to resources and functions but also in terms of travel patterns, social horizons and prevalance of more self-contained local communities.

New town local authorities

10.12 A question arises, therefore, as to the appropriate response to local desires for the creation of new representative structures. In 1854 the legislation allowed for authorities of 1,500 population. In 1878, the Public Health (Ireland) Act created sanitary authorities for towns of over 6,000 population. The town commissioners established in recent years have a population of 8,000 upwards. Against this background and in the light of earlier comments, we are of the view that in today's circumstances, a figure of 7,500 population upwards would be a reasonable minimum level of eligibility for the establishment of a new elective town local authority, given the costs which would fall on taxpayers both at local and national level. It is more likely, but by no means certain, that a town of this size would have an adequate revenue base to justify the creation of a separate local authority. This threshold for potential new authorities does not, in accordance with the factors set out in 10.10, reflect in any way on the position of existing town authorities below that figure.

10.13 In considering specific proposals for the establishment of a new town authority all likely effects would need to be clearly identified, measured against the likely benefits of establishing a local authority and the full implications made known to the people in the town. Such proposals should be assessed by reference to the following factors in particular:

- a thorough assessment of all the financial implications for the town and the county, including the issues referred to at 10.7, 10.8 and 10.9;

- verification that there would be a sufficient revenue base to support a meaningful role for the town authority;

- a clearly established and expressed local public demand;

- full appraisal of the existing position and evaluation of proposed arrangements and consideration of other less formal and costly possibilities as referred to at 10.17 and 10.18.

10.14 The procedures which hitherto governed the creation of new town authorities were prescribed in the Towns Improvement (Ireland) Act, 1854. The powers, procedures and structures provided for in that Act are now largely obsolete and there appears to be general agreement that new criteria and procedures are required (although some of the matters covered in the 1854 Act will still need to be addressed, such as the method of initiating proposals, fixing of boundaries, local consultation/decision, approval of proposals and involvement of the county council). We therefore recommend that procedures along the lines set out in Appendix 10 should apply for the establishment of new town authorities, in towns with a minimum population of 7,500 at the most recent census.

Functions of new town authorities

10.15 Having regard to the population threshold and other criteria proposed, any new authority to be established should exercise a reasonable range of functions and play a meaningful role to the benefit of the town and its residents. However, a new authority would have to develop its role and build up its capacity on a gradual and suitably phased basis, without disruption to the county council's services and organisation. Initially, it would have the same range of functions as the current non-rating authorities, which in accordance with the recommendations in this report would be significantly enhanced, as set out in Chapter 9 especially in the development, social, civic and representational areas. The further expansion of functional responsibilities would involve a process of evolution, including the possible designation of specific functions as discussed in earlier chapters. The Commission is strongly of the view that having regard to the financial issues already outlined, no new separate rating authorities should be established under the existing system of financial relationships between town and county authorities. The appropriate role of any new town authorities would, however, fall to be considered by reference to any new financial arrangements, as discussed in Chapter 15 and any possible changes in the overall system of local government funding which might be introduced following from the current review of local government finance.

Smaller towns

10.16 The aspirations of smaller towns should not be ignored. A new and more flexible framework is required as an alternative to wide scale extension (and in the process, fragmentation) of the formal local government system. It is our view that aspirations for increased town focus, with better public linkage and accessibility, are achievable through better structures of interaction with the county council and without setting up a separate formal local authority. We consider that this represents a more satisfactory and realistic response and crucially, it avoids the fragmentation of resources and organisation, and the expenditure demands inherent in establishing separate fully-fledged formal authorities. This approach can, in appropriate cases, also build on and support community initiatives which have developed locally. A range of measures should be considered to enhance local representation and access to the county council to accommodate particular local circumstances, as follows:

- **County council organisational measures**

  Where there is already a county council presence in the town, this can be upgraded as appropriate. Facilities would be adapted to provide for greater public access and a capacity to deal with a range of queries. Advances in information technology provide increasing potential for improved local contact. Recommendations in Chapter 13 regarding joint services centres would be applicable in appropriate non-local government towns by way of public access points operated by the county council.

- **Voluntary community councils**

  In many non-local authority towns there are various voluntary groups which undertake work for town development, improvement and promotion and of local community and social benefit. These can be accorded recognition through a suitable form of linkage with the local government system to provide a means of direct input in support of local needs and aspirations. The matter of community input and linkage with town authorities is dealt with in Chapter 14. Certain aspects are relevant in the context of non-local authority areas, but it is felt that the latter warrant special procedures, as set out in succeeding paragraphs.

Recognised associations

10.17 In the absence of a formal town local government structure, the following arrangements are recommended for the smaller non-local authority areas as a means of providing enhanced representation and linkage with the local government system:

- Where a local community council, association or similar body is active, the legal framework should provide a system of formal recognition of such body by the county council.

- Recognition should be subject to criteria to establish that the association is properly constituted and reasonably representative.

- There should be a structured system of consultation between representatives of the county council (e.g. the area committee) and those of the recognised association on the lines proposed in Chapter 14 between town authorities and relevant local bodies.

- A recognised association could be afforded representation on any county council committees which may be specifically relevant to its locality. Representatives might also be invited to attend meetings of the county council's area committee where matters of significance to their locality are being dealt with.

- The recognised association should be consulted and kept informed by the county council on matters affecting the town. This should not be confined solely to the fixed cycle of meetings with the association. Local authorities should take a positive, proactive approach, informing the association of relevant proposals and developments on an on-going basis, seeking their views where appropriate and securing their support where possible.

- The recognised association should have a right to propose local projects to be funded through both local contributions and the county council; the interaction in this regard should be a two-way process.

- A specific county council liaison officer should be designated.

- Where the county council has a local office in the town this could be used as a contact point with the association and possibly a venue for meetings and ceremonial functions. The county council might also assist the association by way of accommodation and possibly secretarial backup.

- The recognised local association could, in conjunction with the county council, carry out some of the roles which would be discharged by a town authority for example, in the civic area and possibly, the formulation of a town development programme jointly with the county council. Provision might be made for the county council to delegate specific functions to the association as in the case of existing local government legislation (see 10.18).

10.18 The concept of according recognition to local voluntary groups is not new. The Local Government Acts, 1941 and 1955 provided for "approved local councils", allowed for the delegation of functions to them and for the provision of buildings and other assistance by local authorities. Such broad community involvement is central to recent developments such as LEADER, Area Partnership Companies and County Enterprise Boards. Measures such as those outlined at 10.16 and 10.17 should go a long way to meet the concerns underlying most requests for local authority status and improved relationship with the county council and help to satisfy the desire for some type of ceremonial presence and civic focus for a town.

10.19 While the concept of a recognised local association has been used in reference to non local authority "towns", the latter term need not be applied in a rigid manner. For example, if a local association requests recognition in respect of a wider area (possibly including even neighbouring towns) this need not be excluded in principle. Equally, recognition of quite small centres of population (possibly based on parishes or groups of parishes) should not be excluded where this would be meaningful from a local community viewpoint. It would be desirable, however, that such groupings be compatible with county area sub-divisions and they should not overlap the jurisdiction of town local authorities.

10.20 Having regard to its terms of reference, the fact that local government structures in the Dublin area were the subject of recent reorganisation legislation and given that new arrangements are still in the process of implementation, the Commission confined its review largely to places outside Dublin. It may, at a future point, be desirable to give separate consideration to whether any special sub-county arrangements would be appropriate in the Dublin area. Given the different demographic and physical characteristics of the Dublin conurbation the town-based system is unlikely to be applicable. However, it is possible that the concept of recognised local associations might be relevant in some circumstances.

Chapter 11

Boundaries and Their Implications

This chapter deals with issues relating to town boundaries; section (A) considers the question of boundary definition and section (B) the financial implications of possible boundary extensions.

(A) Town Boundaries

Introduction

11.1   Various aspects of town/county relationships - organisational, functional, financial and territorial - arise in the context of proposals for extension of town boundaries. The issue is often a subject of inter-authority controversy and difficulty. The question of appropriate boundary lines is dealt with in this section. The issue of boundary alteration brings to the fore a number of fundamental questions relating to financial, structural and organisational aspects of local government. The Commission unequivocally favours the establishment of a single rational boundary for every town on a basis which will safeguard the interests of both the town and county authority. However, it is necessary to point out emphatically that in order to achieve this, certain essential prerequisites as regards financial and organisational implications must be met. These are outlined in section B of this chapter. It is also relevant to record that there appears to be an excessive pre-occupation in some cases with boundaries and territorial jurisdiction rather than practical arrangements for optimising services. Inter-authority agreements (subject to decision by the elected members) should be capable of providing suitable arrangements for delivery of services in town environs. The general thrust of this report is to promote cohesiveness, joint approaches and maximisation of the potential of the local government system as a whole. Recommendations to facilitate extension of that approach have been made. We believe that this philosophy, rather than territorial considerations, should also underpin the approach to boundary questions. Boundary issues, per se, tend to be of little or no interest to the public who understandably are concerned with the actual functioning of the overall system and its services and not with what to them may appear to be illogical and unhelpful organisational distinctions.

Formal boundaries and town environs

11.2   The town, as legally defined, is the area for which a town authority is elected and over which it has legal jurisdiction and responsibility for services vested in the authority. [See 11.3 as to the special arrangements introduced for the 1994 town elections.] The legal boundaries of towns were defined in the nineteenth century under various enactments. Boundary alterations have been made on an individual town basis since then, but no general review of town boundaries has been carried out in this century. Many town boundaries have not been adjusted to take account of town growth, leading to a situation where, in effect, continuously built-up parts of the town are located outside of the legal town boundary. For census purposes these are defined as environs. The environs population data shown in the census reports give a very good indication of the scale of boundary overspill problems and of cases where boundary adjustment may need to be considered because the legal boundary has not kept pace with the actual development of the town.

Alterations of areas for electoral purposes under the Local Government Act, 1994

11.3 The 1991 Census identified 62 of the 80 boroughs, urban districts and town commissioners as having environs populations, the aggregate of which was 105,403[1]. In the worst cases the environs population exceeds, or is a significant proportion of, the population within the legal boundary. (Appendix 11 lists these 62 towns). Town elections were held in 1994, on the basis of electoral areas which included people who, despite living outside the administrative town boundaries, were for all intents and purposes residents of the towns. This arrangement applied for electoral purposes only i.e. while the residents in the added areas were eligible to vote in the election of the town authority, the functional jurisdiction of that authority continued unaltered within the original administrative boundary.

11.4 The process for drawing up the 1994 "electoral boundaries" was that the managers of those counties in which the 62 towns with environs populations were situated, submitted proposals, formulated on the basis of specific terms of reference, and put to the elected members of the county and town authorities concerned for decision. The terms of reference indicated that the residential built-up area should be included but areas of largely open land omitted. The emphasis was to define areas for electoral purposes and not necessarily permanent administrative boundaries. Where the elected members agreed to the proposals (56 of the 62 towns concerned) the electoral "boundaries" were extended under the Local Government Act, 1994. In the case of the remaining six, alterations were not sought in five cases[2] while in the sixth[3], local agreement was not recorded between the two authorities concerned.

11.5 Because of the nature of the electoral alterations, not always following townland boundaries, and the lapse in time since the last census, it is impossible to assess with precise accuracy the populations involved in these adjustments. However, if the 56 towns which were extended included say 80% of the environs populations identified in the 1991 Census, the total population of the additional electoral areas would be about 78,000. This, if added to the population within the existing administrative boundaries, would increase the aggregate population of these 56 local authority towns from 337,960 to about 416,000, an increase of about 23%.

11.6 Submissions from many town authorities advocated extension of their administrative jurisdiction to the 1994 electoral areas and some have also sought extension beyond these. The Commission recognises that because the primary emphasis in defining the 1994 areas was for electoral purposes they may not, in all cases, be the most suitable as permanent administrative boundaries. Various issues which arise generally in relation to the definition of town boundary lines are addressed in the following

---

[1] Includes 5,000 cross-county environs population
[2] Ardee, Birr, Clonmel, Droichead Nua, Muinebeag
[3] Ennis

paragraphs. Another separate but crucial factor as regards boundary extension, and especially as regards the extension of functional jurisdiction to the areas defined for electoral purposes in 1994, is the financial implications for the local government system. That issue is dealt with in Section B of this chapter.

Town boundary definition

11.7   The Commission is in no doubt that in defining town areas the built-up area of the town proper should be included within the town boundary. In most cases this will include some or most of the census environs (but not necessarily all) if boundaries of reasonable configuration and definition are to apply. This approach follows from the rejection of previous proposals for a new system of larger town-based areas encompassing the wider hinterland, in favour of the existing more narrowly defined town-only authority system. The definition of the town is consequently to be based on the continuous built-up town area - the town proper - but not including the wider rural hinterland or separated urban pockets. In stating this fact, the Commission is merely reflecting the parameters set by its terms of reference and not expressing a judgement as to whether this is the most appropriate unit or as to the suitability or otherwise of other units with comprehensive territorial coverage which are the norm throughout Western Europe.

11.8   In defining suitable town boundaries the Commission is of the view that the following considerations should apply:

- Insofar as possible the town proper - the entire continuously built up area - should come within a single boundary which should apply for all purposes. Well-removed, isolated pockets, and dispersed and extended lines of ribbon development should be omitted.

- The boundary should be of suitable overall configuration, taking account of planning and service requirements, and should provide a suitable area in terms of organisation of services and discharge of functions.

- Boundary lines should be drawn so as to avoid the creation of service, financial or other anomalies and public confusion e.g. due to boundaries running along roads fronted by development on opposite sides in different jurisdictions.

- Financial implications must be considered - see 11.11 and section (B). In some instances under the current system of two entirely separate revenue raising authorities, this has caused certain areas of commercial property and adjoining housing which, for all practical purposes form part of the town proper, to be retained as part of the county, notwithstanding that criteria such as those above would suggest their inclusion within the town boundary.

11.9   If the criterion that the entire built-up area should form the town administrative area is accepted, a number of issues arise in relation to current town boundaries as follows:

(a) Some towns are currently divided by county boundaries, with parts of what is a single urban settlement located in different counties and one part outside of the town boundary. Appendix 12 contains a list of such towns. It seems clear that the division of functional responsibilities for what is a single urban centre is inherently inefficient and also hampers the integrated planning of the town.

(b) Some towns where the electoral boundary was not altered in 1994 have environs population outside the administrative boundary and some outward extension is likely to be warranted.

(c) The 1994 electoral revision process produced, in some instances areas of unsatisfactory configuration e.g. long fingers of ribbon development omitting backlands and giving a "star" shape to the town, with consequent problems for normal administrative purposes such as service provision, development planning and control.

11.10 Arising from the foregoing, the following principles should apply in defining town boundaries, subject to the resolution of the general financial and organisational issues dealt with in section (B) under:

(a) County boundaries should be adjusted so that entire town areas come under the jurisdiction of one authority for service and planning purposes.

(b) The boundaries of towns with substantial environs population, not included in the 1994 electoral revision, should encompass the area of the town proper.

(c) While in many cases the 1994 electoral areas will be suitable, in some cases the configuration of these would not provide satisfactory permanent administrative boundaries to overcome difficulties of the sort referred to at 11.9(c) above.

(d) In the case of the relatively small number of towns experiencing rapid population growth town boundaries should be kept under review in the light of census results.

11.11 The points at 11.10 are objective principles but a decision to undertake revision of administrative boundaries must be based on full assessment of likely implications. There are 41 town rating authorities in 19 counties where electoral "boundaries" were extended in 1994. The possibility of extending the permanent administrative boundaries of these towns raises major issues. Boundary alteration on this scale will affect the local government system as a whole in the counties concerned. Boundary alteration involves consequential effects on all of the authorities concerned - if the town authority gains, the county council must lose (in some cases more than the former gains).

(B)   Financial and Organisational Implications of Boundary Alteration

Implications of current financial arrangements

11.12 As will become evident, there are significant difficulties with the implementation of boundary alterations due particularly to the existence of two separate revenue-raising jurisdictions within the county while at the same time the county council has significant responsibilities in the urban areas as well as in the non-urban parts of the county. The matter is exacerbated by the complexity of financial relationships between town and county authorities and variations in local resources.

11.13 The financial base of local government generally is limited in terms of local revenue sources. It was suggested to the Commission that difficulties in this regard have arisen because the buoyancy of revenue sources generally has not kept pace with increases in financial requirements (which have, it is claimed, tended to run ahead of the general inflation rate) and a significant proportion of local authority expenditure is non-discretionary. The relative strength or weakness of the local revenue base varies between counties, depending particularly on factors such as the extent of commercial valuation, number of service charge payers and buoyancy of development and commercial activity which can produce revenue spin-offs of various kinds. The revenue base constraints are heightened by a system of local financial arrangements in which there are separate revenue-raising authorities located within the county. Where there is a strong revenue base within a town, the potential revenue is available to the town authority in the first instance and this can be reflected in either relatively high standards of service, relatively low levels of rates and charges, or a balance between the two. The county council is responsible for a significant range of services within towns. It does not have direct access to the revenue base within the town to fund these. It is dependant on a complex system of revenue transfers from the urban authorities which are designed to achieve an equitable and effective sharing of costs between the different town areas and the county. The effectiveness of this system (the county demand), which was devised on the basis of rates yield, appears to be somewhat uncertain in current circumstances.

11.14 Fragmentation of the overall local revenue base (which is already limited in some counties), into separate units for revenue raising purposes does not promote maximisation of revenue generation or optimisation of its distribution. Extension of administrative (and under present arrangements, fiscal) boundaries is likely to worsen this situation. This is particularly so because the county councils are, in many cases, dependent on revenue buoyancy in the environs of certain towns to sustain their overall financial responsibilities (including support for weaker town authorities). In the longer term, boundary extensions could lead to loss of buoyancy for a county council, because a significant proportion of future development is likely to occur in the town environs. Such a development could progressively curtail the potential financial capacity of county councils, with consequent damage to the local government system as a whole. If alteration of administrative boundaries is to proceed, it may be necessary to remove the element of fragmentation from local financial arrangements so as to maximise the potential revenue available to the local service as a whole, accompanied by procedures to achieve equitable distribution of revenue yield.

Key issues in boundary alteration

11.15 Among the considerations which arise in the context of possible boundary extensions are:

(a) The town authority must have the capacity, including financial, organisational and other resources, to carry out its responsibilities properly and efficiently both in the existing and added areas.

(b) The extension of the town authority's functional jurisdiction should not result in any seriously adverse financial impact: on the town itself (for example in terms of the cost of carrying out functions in the added area compared to additional revenue accruing from the added area); on the county (if the revenue base in the added area was significantly greater than the cost of providing services which would transfer to the town authority); or on any other town authorities (if net loss of revenue to the county council reduced its capacity to assist weaker town authorities).

(c) Where extension of urban jurisdiction results in a net loss of revenue to the county council or net extra cost to the town authority, this raises the question of compensatory transfers between the authorities or other financial adjustments. Such on-going circular payments might call into question the allocation of responsibilities for revenue-raising and distribution.

(d) From comments made in submissions it seems likely that savings to the county council in expenditure in the environs will not match the expenditure seen as necessary by the town authority to accelerate investment in the added area - for services such as roads, footpaths, lighting, amenities, etc. to an equivalent town level.

(e) The organisational implications (and associated costs) of transferring significant blocks of work from the county council to town authorities must be taken into account. As indicated in Chapters 9 and 10 in relation to town commissioners and possible new town authorities, the extra cost (especially in terms of staff requirements and overheads) to a relatively small authority of taking on significant extra functions is likely to exceed the reduction in cost to the much larger county authority shedding these functions for part of its area. The addition of the environs population to some towns would represent population increases of 100% and more. Existing staff complements can be low (e.g. less than 20 in one town which would experience a population increase of around 3,000) and existing budgets only a fraction of the county council level. It is most unlikely that the saving to the county would be sufficient to match the additional requirements of the town authority. Moreover, the reduced county council organisation is likely to be less cost effective relative to its remaining area of responsibility.

(f) It is difficult to justify significant additional costs (which would ultimately fall to be met by the public by way of taxation or other charges either locally or nationally) arising solely from rearrangement of territorial responsibilities among two public bodies. In this connection, many of the submissions from local authorities advocated additional funding from central level to support boundary revision.

11.16 Extension of a town authority's functional jurisdiction must not result in reduced effectiveness, efficiency or economy in the discharge of functions; there must be no avoidable increases in financial demands on the Exchequer or local authorities; staff numbers should not increase unnecessarily. The Commission is legally obliged to have regard to these criteria under the Local Government Act, 1994. That Act also requires us to address the question of consequential implications for county councils and to have regard to the need to safeguard the position of the county councils as the primary units of local government. We do not interpret the latter phrase as implying any general control or supervisory position in relation to town authorities. Rather we understand the primacy of the county council to relate to the structural, organisational and fiscal aspects of the local government system. The county council has significant responsibilities throughout the county and, in practice, performs an overall supporting and balancing role, particularly in relation to relatively weak sub-areas. Equally our brief to propose satisfactory arrangements for local government in towns carries an obligation to ensure that boundary alteration does not result in a net additional burden on towns which would adversely affect their capacity and viability. These requirements must be brought fully to bear and kept in sight at all times in assessing the effects of boundary alteration.

Specific implications of boundary alteration

11.17 Within the present local authority financial system, town boundary alteration clearly has significant financial implications. The factors within the system which give rise to this have been outlined in general terms above. The more specific implications are outlined hereunder:

11.17.1 Rates

Rates are paid only on commercial property. In many towns there are significant pockets of industrial/commercial development in the environs of towns. With the transfer of this territory from the county to the town, rates income generated by such property also transfers to the town authority. Furthermore, there are differing rate levels between town and county. Where the town rate is lower, the transfer will mean a reduction in the total combined income generated by both authorities - in other words a leakage of money from the system. Where town rates are higher the increases will, in some cases, need to be introduced on a suitably phased basis to avoid sharp increases. During this period the town authority would not, therefore, have the benefit of the full potential rate yield in the added area.

11.17.2 Service charges

A similar situation applies in relation to commercial and domestic service charges, currently paid in the environs to the county council in respect of refuse, water and sewerage. Under the current system where the territory transfers, this income is lost to the county. There are significant charge differentials in some cases which would with present arrangements, involve significant leakage of revenue from the system. [See Chapter 8 as to recommendations in relation to water services].

11.17.3 Grants and and other income

The transfer of territory could also involve a readjustment of rate support grant and of non-national road grants from the county council to the town authority. Other losses/gains would arise from: income generated by planning application fees; development levies paid pursuant to conditions attached to planning permissions; the transfer of local authority houses and other minor charges related to graveyards and other facilities in the added area.

11.17.4 Expenditure and income recovery

There will be reductions in county council expenditure on services arising from the transfer of territory. However, as indicated already, savings will not, in practice, be fully realisable in many cases because of indivisabilities and other scale related factors in the county organisation. There will be some recovery of revenue to the county council by way of an increased county demand (that demand is related to the relative total valuations of town and county - see Appendix 13). These savings and increases in income have to be offset against the income loss referred to in the previous paragraphs to determine the net overall effect on the county. As against any revenue increase for the town authority, there will be increased expenditure arising from the provision of services to meet demands for higher standards. Moreover, for the reasons already noted on the county council side, the necessary staff and other resources may not transfer fully to the town authority.

11.17.5 Long term effects

In many instances, future commercial development is likely to be concentrated in the added areas. This, therefore, is where buoyancy in the rating base arising from additional valuations is likely to be concentrated along with any other property-related income. In the longer term, therefore, there could, without appropriate adjustments, be a continuing loss of prospective income to the county. This could have the effect of limiting its potential development and its general supportive role as the primary local government unit. In many cases therefore, without appropriate adjustments, the overall end result could be significant dislocation of potential resources. This could, over time, significantly constrain not only the strategic development capacity of many county councils but their ability to sustain the weaker elements of the system.

Sample impact assessments

11.18   The Commission, conscious of the foregoing, was aware that local authorities generally had not themselves carried out assessments. A small group of local authority officials was asked to consider, inter alia, the likely effects of possible boundary extensions (based on the 1994 electoral areas) on a number of local authorities. They reported as follows:-

The impact varies from town to town and from county to county. In general, however, the critical factor is whether there is substantial commercial development in the proposed added area. The additional rating income available to the urban authority in such cases would generally be adequate to fund the additional expenditure arising, but the loss of rates income to the county council could be significant, particularly if there are no other substantial towns in the county health district. In the ten towns looked at, there would be a net loss to the county in eight cases.

Where the proposed added area consists of mainly residential properties, the extra income accruing to the urban authority would be insufficient to fund the extra cost of services. In such cases the net loss to the county council is much less significant than in cases where there is substantial commercial development.

In cases involving substantial boundary extensions, there is likely to be a net increase in staffing requirements - the extra requirements in the urban authority may not be fully met by transfer/redeployment from the county council. There could also be additional accommodation requirements for the urban authority, if not located in the same building as county council offices.

In general, there would be an expectation of a higher standard of services in an added area than that being provided by a county council in the area prior to extension. This would apply in areas such as local authority housing maintenance, provision of footpaths, public lighting, parks and open spaces, street cleaning and refuse collection.

In the majority of cases, service charges are lower in urban areas than in county health districts. Where a boundary is extended, there would be significant pressure to apply the lower charges in the added area.

The above assessment employed a standard methodology. Accordingly, the resultant figures might be subject to some adjustment to take full account of individual variations. Nonetheless, the Commission is satisfied that its general thrust and overall conclusions are fundamentally valid.

Conclusions

11.19   Our interim appraisal of the position regarding the problems of discrepancy between administrative and electoral areas was that the existing borough corporations would constitute the only category of town authority potentially suitable for consideration in this regard in the short-term; this opinion was formed without the benefit of financial impact assessments. Further, we saw changes being contingent on satisfactory arrangements between the local authorities concerned. In this regard we were mindful, in particular, of the fact that borough corporations constitute a discrete category of local authorities, all of which were likely to have a sufficiently strong organisational base on which to build the necessary additional capacity. However, the results of the subsequent assessments indicated that the severity of financial impact in particular cases is likely to be greater than might have been anticipated. Even though this may not be so in all cases, the cumulative effect of a general programme of boundary extensions could impact adversely both on particular counties and on the local government system as a whole. In some cases where boundary extension would not impact adversely on the county council it could, conversely, do so on the town authority where the "added area" does not bring a revenue base to match the cost of services. In the course of our consultations it was also emphasised that, as well as direct financial impact, transfer of jurisdiction from the county council to town authorities could, in some cases, cause significant organisational disruption and consequent diseconomies and loss of cost-effectiveness. In this regard, the group which carried out assessments for the Commission suggested that a unified staff structure within each county would help to alleviate the problem of likely additional staff costs which might arise due to changes in functional jurisdiction. Another factor which emerged was that implications of change in local authority revenue jurisdiction at the present time could pose subsequent difficulty in the event of significant change arising from the overall review of local government finance which is currently underway.

11.20   The Commission is of the view that:

- the administrative area of a town authority should encompass the entire town area, with town authorities having functional responsibility in keeping with their capabilities and where appropriate, joint arrangements or agreements being used to ensure the most effective service delivery;

- an outcome of boundary adjustment which leads to a significant loss of resources for counties together with other possible financial or organisational difficulties as already outlined, would be contrary to the objective of maintaining the county as the primary unit of local government and in the longer term, could weaken the local government system as a whole;

There is a need, therefore, to strike a balance between adverse financial effects and appropriate transfer of jurisdiction to the town authority. In our view this cannot be done without a fundamental reappraisal of the current local government financial arrangements. In the present system, these objectives are difficult to reconcile. Boundary extensions tend (to differing degrees in different circumstances) to increase the problem of fragmentation and thereby weaken the overall financial base. We recommend, accordingly, that a further phase of the study of local authority finance should give specific attention to the question of an appropriate new system of town/county financial inter-linkage. We give further consideration to this in Chapter 15 which deals with the general question of financial arrangements between town and county authorities.

11.21   This issue is separate from the examination of the overall requirements of local government funding or alternative methods of funding local authorities. It is, however, related to such matters in two ways. Firstly, it is desirable that any new overall system of local government funding which might emerge should be applied on the basis of a rational and effective system of "internal" financial arrangements between town and county authorities. Secondly, there is a danger that a possible alternative local authority revenue system having particular local incidence could have a seriously adverse impact in the event of wide scale boundary extensions, with severe impact on the county council's revenue base and further distortion and dislocation in the local government revenue system generally.

11.22 Our review has brought to light significant difficulties with boundary extensions generally, as outlined in preceding paragraphs. We consider it essential to make these issues as clear as possible. However, we are anxious to take a positive approach on this issue, particularly in view of the apparent expectation, especially on the part of some town authority members, that developments in this regard may be possible in the reasonably short term. We have, therefore, given much thought to how progress might be initiated, notwithstanding the constraints which apply. Consideration could be given to addressing the position of those areas added for electoral purposes in the case of borough corporations and the small number of other authorities where administrative (and not simply electoral) boundary alteration proposals had previously been formulated and agreed by the local authorities concerned and which ipso facto were seen to not adversely affect the county. Such action would have to be considered in the light of likely implications, long term as well as short term and on the basis that, in the longer term, financial relationships between town and county authorities will be governed by revised arrangements emerging from the overall review of finance.

11.23 The financial implications of any jurisdictional alterations in the short-term of the type referred to at 11.22 will need to be carefully assessed and accurately quantified on a case by case basis by the local authorities concerned. Local arrangements would need to provide for functional and organisational, as well as financial, adjustments. It is not feasible to formulate a standard framework for such arrangements which would be universally applicable, because of local variations, not only on the revenue side but also in relation to matters such as organisational arrangements for provision of services, inter-authority agreements in that regard and associated financial arrangements. What are likely to be called for are ad hoc arrangements tailored specifically to meet the particular local circumstances. Among the matters arising for consideration in that context would be the question of inter-authority payments; rate and service charge levels; organisational or service delivery adjustments and allocation of current rate support grant levels. It may be necessary in individual cases to utilise some or all of these means to devise an appropriate satisfactory outcome for both authorities. The determination of whether such an outcome is feasible is dependent on the necessary detailed financial analysis. Any ad hoc transfers or adjustments arising in this context should not be seen as providing a basis for long-term financial arrangements generally. They would be purely short-term measures to enable boundary alterations of this type to proceed pending implementation of a revised system of financial arrangements between town and county authorities generally and clarification of possible changes in local authority revenue sources.

11.24 All other cases should await the implementation of a new system of financial inter-relationship, and clarification of the position arising from the review of local government finance. The organisational implications of boundary alteration referred to already, reinforce the need to achieve a more integrated staff and organisational structure as recommended in Chapter 12. While there may be some instances in which the impact, on either the town or county authorities involved, of extending the administrative boundary to coincide with the electoral area might not appear significant in the short term (for example, if the area or valuation involved is small), such cases do not justify the undertaking of a general programme of boundary extension in advance of the necessary changes in

89

financial and organisational arrangements referred to above. The fact that longer term implications, even in such cases, could be significant, reinforces this point.

Practical arrangements for services locally

11.25 In the case of towns where the boundary would not be altered pending developments in relation to financial arrangements, we consider that many of the concerns of local authority members regarding discrepancy between the administrative boundary and the additional electoral area can be met as follows:

- the joint structures recommended in Chapter 12 should help to eliminate anomalies and discrepancies which may currently exist arising from separate local authority jurisdictions in the towns and environs; in particular, the town clerk and other staff will be better positioned to pursue issues generally on behalf of elected members and the public;

- joint services centres proposed in Chapter 13 should help to alleviate difficulties experienced by the public in relation to separate jurisdictions;

- the town improvement programme proposed in Chapter 6 should achieve a more integrated approach in relation to the town and environs and these, together with the increased interaction at elected member level proposed in Chapter 12, should enable town authority members to have greater input to and influence over decisions relating to county council services in the town and environs;

- where appropriate, formal agreements can be made (e.g. under section 59 of the Local Government Act, 1955 or any new provisions) to enable the town authority to take on responsibility for services in the environs, as is already the case in some instances; or to make other practical arrangements for service delivery.

In the course of our review it became apparent to us that the essential issue in many cases is not the formal definition of boundaries per se - although the issue is commonly expressed as such - but rather practical considerations of particular functions within a town being exercised by different authorities in different parts of the one town with consequent variations in service levels and attendant confusion and frustration on the part of the public and elected members. The approaches outlined by us should go a long way towards addressing the situation. As stated at the outset, it is our objective to promote cohesiveness, maximisation of the use of resources and optimisation of the service provided by the overall local government system. We also accept that it is necessary to achieve appropriate administrative boundaries without financial or organisational disruption. These objectives require, not a concentration on territorial jurisdiction but more a focus on the melting away of organisational and attitudinal barriers in the interests of achieving greater overall effectiveness and quality of service

Part
4

An Effective and Cohesive Local Service

Chapter 12

Town/County Linkage

This chapter recommends new joint arrangements between town and county authorities at both staff and elected member level to underpin the effective discharge of functions and provision of service to the public.

Introduction

12.1 The recommendations in Part 2 provide the opportunity for a significant future role for town local government. This is in marked contrast to previous reports, prepared within different parameters, which proposed the abolition of, or restriction of the role of, town authorities. The future role now envisaged involves new areas of activity, increased emphasis on some existing areas and re-defined roles in what might be termed the traditional mainstream local authority functions. There should be reduction in overlapping or ambiguity of roles between town and county authorities.

A more cohesive local service

12.2 The Commission is required to make proposals as to:

- financial, staffing and organisational matters in respect of town authorities; and

- consequential implications for county councils of its proposals and the appropriate relationships between town authorities and county councils.

These issues and the question of town authority functions, are closely related. The role proposed for town authorities can only be sustained through a more unified overall local service. At operational level, there must be joint staffing and organisational arrangements. Recommendations for this, and for greater interaction between elected members are set out in this chapter. More unified financial arrangements between town and county authorities are also essential to underpin a substantial future role for town authorities, particularly in the context of possible boundary extensions. Issues and recommendations in that regard are set out in Chapter 15. A further important positive effect of a more unified approach is that it will facilitate a more integrated, comprehensive and accessible service to the public which is a fundamental objective of this review. Recommendations for that purpose are set out at Chapter 13.

12.3 We are also conscious of the relationship between this review and that of the Devolution Commission and the review of local government finance. The recommendations in this chapter and those in Chapter 15 regarding financial relationships, will help to achieve more rational and effective internal arrangements and operations in the local government system which should in turn be beneficial in the implementation of proposals emanating from these other reviews.

Issues involved

12.4   In many cases town and county authorities operate well together. However, the degree of separation inherent in the system, with separate organisations and elected councils, can on occasion, promote fragmentation. This can occur despite the best efforts of all concerned to achieve communication and co-ordination. It is more a reflection of the structural divisions within the system than deficiencies on the part of personnel at either level. There is need to promote greater cohesiveness, effectiveness and coherence in the overall local public service.

12.5   During the course of its review the Commission encountered variations in the quality of relationships between town and county authorities. In some cases there appears to be quite a high degree of co-operation, co-ordination and communication. In others these features are less developed. In some instances there appears, on the part of town authorities, to be a sense of inadequate awareness of and input to county council activities, and possibly a degree of friction between the two levels.

12.6   The type of specific problems identified, by town authorities in particular, include the following:

* Perceived difficulty on the part of town authority members in having queries or proposals pursued relating to matters in the town which are county council responsibilities.

* Perceived difficulty on the part of town authority members in obtaining adequate information on county council plans, proposals and activities; surprisingly, this and the previous point, appear to arise even in areas where there is overlap between town and county authority membership.

* Confusion, inconvenience and difficulty to the public and the elected members, particularly in relation to matters such as roads and housing, in which some aspects are the responsibility of the town authority and others the county council. A particular source of irritation cited to the Commission is connection to the public water or sewerage network involving separate roads and sanitary authorities. The public might reasonably expect to be able to deal with a single local government agency in such a matter. Similarly, where different authorities are responsible for the cleaning of adjacent streets in a town the public have understandable difficulty in grasping the jurisdictional distinctions.

* Alleged insufficiency of emphasis on the part of the county council in relation to town matters while, conversely, the county council may point to the need to view issues within a broader county framework.

* Concern about difficulty in maintaining continuity of suitable staff at town clerk level in smaller authorities, with staff movement on promotion after relatively short periods. It was suggested that, ideally, a town clerk assignment should apply for a minimum of two years. Lack of lateral mobility at town clerk level between town and county authorities was seen as having adverse

effects both in terms of personal career development and difficulty in retaining staff.

- Inability of residents of towns away from the county town (i.e. the county council headquarters location) to transact, or initiate business with the local authority system (town or county) locally. This applies also to residents of the county area adjacent to the town who are currently obliged to deal directly with the county council office on all local authority matters.

Functional responsibility and operational arrangements

12.7 The degree of separation between the town and county organisations, affecting both elected members and the public also has fundamental implications for the efficiency or otherwise of the allocation of functions between town and county authorities. In Chapter 8 a degree of redistribution of certain infrastructural and regulatory functions between town and county authorities is recommended, on grounds of the requirements of certain functions relative to the capacity and resources of local authorities. However, for services such as housing, roads and planning, parallel responsibility will remain. If this involved the maintenance of duplicate operational capacities, it would be open to serious question on grounds of overall efficiency and optimal use of public resources.

12.8 Duplication is reduced in practice because some town authorities utilise county resources to discharge certain functions. The pooling of operational resources on a wider scale is required. This will maximise efficiency, by ensuring that town authorities, especially those with limited resources, have access to the capacity needed to discharge their functions effectively. It will ensure that the best possible standard of service is provided to the public and that the elected members are in a position to represent them well. Joint approaches have already been recommended for particular functions in Part 2, including a joint programme approach in relation to town development and other activities. Such approaches will be facilitated by greater co-operation, co-ordination and cohesiveness between town and county authorities in terms of staffing, organisation and linkage between elected members. Recommendations to that end are set out in succeeding paragraphs.

Joint staffing and organisational arrangements

12.9 The Commission fully acknowledges the commitment and effort of both town and county members and staff. Changes recommended in this chapter are designed to help them to carry out their functions more effectively. However, in order to provide the optimum public service and most efficient use of resources there is a need for some adjustment in the present arrangements. We recommend a pooling of the staffing and organisational aspects of town and county authorities, subject to deployment by the manager throughout the authorities in the county. There would continue to be a body of staff assigned to deal with services in the town area. Where town authorities currently have their own engineering staff, this arrangement would not be adversely affected. Indeed the town engineering function should be enhanced by greater integration with the county engineering staff in respect of the wider area, with deployment being a matter for decision by local management. Under the joint arrangement proposed, the town authority would enjoy access to increased staff resources, with the possibility of additional staff being deployed from the wider county area, as necessary, to meet exigencies. The possibility of flexible deployment would operate in both directions to the mutual advantage of town and county authorities. Full account would, of course need to be taken of human resources factors in deployment of staff. By developing joint town/area services centres, both town and county area services should be facilitated, while optimising the use of the total available resources.

12.10 Under the new arrangement the county council would fulfil employment formalities in respect of all staff in the joint service. The county council would be best positioned to provide the overall personnel function and related services. The proposed assignment would not restrict open recruitment to town clerk posts; indeed the overall practical effect should be to widen the field of potential recruits to such posts. Staff in the joint structure assigned to town duties would report to the town clerk who would have overall responsibility for the joint town/area office. The title of the post should also be adapted in accordance with the changed role. The title "town clerk" derives from an era when the emphasis of the role was significantly different to what is now envisaged. A title such as "administrator" might better reflect the role proposed in relation to the recommended joint structure.

12.11 The terms and conditions of existing staff members should not be affected by the proposed arrangements per se, save in accordance with any changes implemented through normal procedures. There would be positive effects both for staff (including town clerks and other grades) and for the local authorities concerned. The proposed arrangement would allow for full mobility within a single cohesive staffing framework within the county. This would make assignment to town clerk posts more attractive to staff generally and at the same time facilitate organisational effectiveness. It would allow enhanced scope for career development and assignment of staff in accordance with abilities and suitability. In this regard, it was suggested to us that the particular nature of the town clerk's role places special demands on personal suitability and qualities such as commitment and initiative. Equally, service in the post of town clerk can provide valuable experience for future career development, as the duties carry a significant degree of individual responsibility for the overall running of the authority along with close contact with the elected members, the public and other organisations. The need for continuity should also be taken into account in assignment to town clerk posts as should the desirability of minimising delay in the filling of vacancies.

12.12 A particular advantage envisaged under the proposed arrangement is that all administrative staff would, as part of a joint town/county structure, have access to the county council organisation and be in a position to pursue all matters relating to the town in that context. The town clerk should, accordingly, be in a position to report to the town authority members on matters generally affecting the town.

12.13 The proposed joint staffing/organisation structure would not affect the respective powers and functions of any of the authorities concerned or the policy or decision-making capacities of their elected members. It would not, per se, alter the financial responsibilities or powers of the authorities.

Rather, it should enable all town authorities to have access to the resources necessary to discharge such functions as effectively as possible, while at the same time helping to overcome many of the deficiencies already noted.

12.14 There are already specific elements of integration in the local government system. For example, the county manager is also manager for each town authority in the county. Engineering services have, for the most part, been integrated. There are procedures for recruitment of clerical staff through a common pool and there is, generally, lateral mobility at that level between town and county authorities. There is already a degree of de facto operational integration to the extent that in many cases town authority functions are carried out through the operational resources and expertise of the county council. What is now proposed would extend and generalise this integrated approach, leading to a unified local service of which the town clerk would be an integral part in the joint operational organisation for the town area. Details of any consequential changes in administrative procedures (e.g. accounting, personnel, etc) would be worked out in the context of the reorganisation implementation process.

Development of joint arrangements

12.15 While the initial emphasis in the establishment of the necessary joint arrangements would be on the staff role, over time there should be integration of other resources and assets. This would facilitate flexibility in the deployment of the total resources of the local government service and maximise operational efficiency generally. This will require general organisational adaptation. The area organisational sub-divisions of the county will need to focus on the towns to facilitate co-ordination with the town authority. Currently, most area offices of county councils are largely engineering-related, with only a small and relatively junior staff complement and little or no public access. It is understood that some county councils are currently in the process of upgrading and extending their area offices. We recommend that such developments be pursued in conjunction with the establishment of the proposed joint staff/organisation structure. Pilot studies may be useful to guide implementation of the revised arrangements. Realistically, adaptation and implementation of the complete joint organisational arrangement will be gradual. Nonetheless, over the medium-term, significant progress can and should, be made.

12.16 Implementation of the proposed arrangements will, to some extent, be a matter of opportunity. It is critical that all future accommodation needs, or proposals for change in existing arrangements for town or county, follow a pattern leading to the placement of staff within a single building or complex to facilitate a cohesive local service in the public interest. In many cases this will involve the merger of the county area office and the town authority office to provide a single joint services centre. This would not be concerned exclusively or mainly with engineering or infrastructural matters, but should have a role across a broad range of local authority functions with particular emphasis on facilitating access by the public. Specific recommendations in that regard are contained in Chapter 13.

12.17 The integrated approach can extend to former town commissioners and thus allow the possibility of a degree of enhancement of their structures (e.g. through upgrading of the county council area office as a joint facility) which would not otherwise be feasible. The allocation of staff or other resources in such cases would be a matter for consideration by local management in each case. With the exception of a part-time town clerk in a few instances, town commissioners do not have their own staff at present. Support - mainly to service meetings - is usually provided by the county council. However, a number of county council area offices and a few county council headquarters are located in town commissioner towns. This can provide the basis for developments on the lines already proposed.

The ethos of a joint service

12.18 As well as organisational changes, the proposals in this chapter will necessitate the development of a new approach on the part of staff assigned to town and county authorities alike. Personnel in the new joint service will have to see themselves as serving the public and the elected members in relation to all matters affecting the town. This will include, as far as possible, matters for which the county has legal responsibility but which members of the public and indeed elected members, might regard simply as local government services or issues. Legalistic aspects of functional jurisdiction as between different categories of authorities should impinge on the public as little as possible. It is essential that staff are not operating in isolation or at cross purposes but rather that there is a spirit and approach of cohesiveness with a view to maximising efficiency and quality of service. All staff must see their role in the context of an overall local government team, serving the needs of local communities, elected members and the public. For example, the relevant administrative and technical staff would deal with matters raised by town council members in relation to both town and county functions. For those who receive services, divisions between town and county authorities are largely irrelevant and generally incomprehensible. The establishment of a unified staff structure is an essential requirement in this context.

12.19 The proposed joint structures should lead to a significantly enhanced, integrated total service to the public in the context of a more decentralised county administration. As this goes to the heart of the Commission's primary objectives, as outlined in the introduction to the report, this aspect of the organisational proposals is dealt with further in Chapter 13. Meanwhile, a further element in the establishment of a more cohesive and co-ordinated approach between town and county authorities, viz enhanced interaction at elected member level, is considered in the remaining paragraphs of this chapter.

Linkage between elected members

12.20 The elected members occupy the pre-eminent position in local government. It is our view that in a re-vitalised system of town local government, they should play an even more active and visible leadership role. A primary objective of this review is to promote the best possible quality of democratic representation. To secure this objective and to achieve the necessary cohesiveness between town and county authorities, it is essential that there be adequate linkage and co-operation between the respective sets of elected members. Such arrangements already exist in many areas: for example, periodic joint meetings between town members and members of county council area committees and arrangements for the provision of information on county council matters to town authority members. This is not universal practice. Interaction between town and county members needs to be improved in some cases and there is need to extend best practice to all areas, with a more formal underpinning of joint arrangements.

12.21 A structured system of periodic formal meetings between town and county members is recommended in all areas, a procedure which is already standard practice in some places. This would involve the area committee of the county council or, where such a committee does not exist, a delegation of county council members representative of the general town area. These meetings would constitute joint fora with county and town members meeting as equals. We recommend the holding of such meetings on a quarterly basis and that they should be mandatory.

12.22 The proposed meetings would serve a consultative and informational role particularly for town members in relation to county council functions. Town members would be able to put forward views in relation to county council activities affecting the town. It would also provide a context in which joint initiatives involving substantive decisions of policy and finance could be dealt with, such as the adoption of the proposed joint town improvement programme and proposals for agreements relating to the discharge of functions; subject to any subsequent formal ratification. These joint fora would also help to maintain general oversight of the process of co-ordination and integration with particular reference to the development of joint services centres. Our proposals for greater operational and representational cohesiveness would also enhance the effectiveness of town councils by giving improved access to the overall county organisation and support for the enhanced town authority role in areas such as development and social and civic activities recommended in Part 2.

12.23 We also recommend that, where necessary, the county electoral areas be adjusted to a more town-focused configuration to reflect natural hinterlands and population trends. This would also facilitate the recommended interaction between town and county members. This might be considered in the context of any review of local electoral areas to take account of the 1996 census returns.

12.24 We also considered, as a further means of improving linkage between town and county authorities, the possiblility of a representative (for example the chairperson) or representatives of the town authority being nominated to membership of the county council. We know that there is some opposition to this suggestion even from town authority members whom we met during the course of our review. The general feeling appears to be that it would not be appropriate for persons who had not been elected to the council to be nominated to it by another body. Another suggestion, that town authority members might attend county council meetings in an observer capacity with a view to reporting back to their council, was thought unlikely to be effective. The Commission has, on balance, decided against recommending any such procedures and is confident that the recommendations made in this report to enhance linkage between town and county members will, if fully implemented, have the desired effect.

12.25 We consider that greater interaction and co-ordination at elected member level is vital to the achievement of a coherent and outward-looking approach throughout the local government system. Where such interaction exists at present it is reported to be very productive especially when combined with integration or co-operation in engineering services. The joint programme approach recommended in relation to various functional areas in Part 2 and the system of integrated public service recommended in Chapter 13, accompanied by the more complete organisational cohesiveness recommended in this chapter, will we believe, lead to considerable benefit in terms of quality and efficiency of service and effectiveness of representation.

Strategy for development of co-ordination and joint arrangements

12.26 The various measures proposed for co-operation, co-ordination and joint arrangements between town and county authorities will involve action on a number of fronts - staffing, organisational, elected member and associated functional/financial adjustments. Some aspects will require a period of time for implementation. The process will clearly require a considerable degree of planning. It is important, however, that the process is launched as soon as possible. We consider, therefore, that an appropriate context within which to pursue the matter would be the Strategic Management Initiative (SMI) which is already being implemented in Departments of State and is now being extended to other areas of the public service, including local authorities. In March 1996, the Minister for the Environment asked county councils and county boroughs to begin their formal involvement in the SMI by preparing strategy statements for their own organisations. County council strategic management plans would provide an appropriate initial general context to address the issues.

12.27 We recommend that, in conjunction with the establishment of the proposed joint operational structures, there should also be a comprehensive review in each county of the allocation, as between the county council and town authorities, of responsibilities, particularly in the infrastructural and regulatory areas dealt with in Chapter 8. Such a review would make it possible to confirm or alter any existing agency or joint arrangements, or establish such arrangements in further areas where required. The strategic roles of the town and county authorities within the overall local service in each county could thus be defined in the light of local circumstances and the strengths, weaknesses, resources and capacities of the respective authorities.

12.28 As part of the overall reform process, time frames for initiation and completion of implementation of the arrangements proposed in this Part should be set (in the context of SMI or otherwise). Arrangements should be subject to ongoing review, having regard inter alia to any relevant matters arising from the Devolution Commission's review and the study on local government finance, as well as ongoing developments in the future. We recommend, however, that steps to implement the proposed arrangements for a joint town/county staffing structure should be initiated as soon as possible.

12.29 Finally, it is essential that personnel, both staff and elected members, be involved as fully as possible in the implementation of the new arrangements. They must be fully informed of the purpose and implications of the new arrangements. Furthermore, there must be a positive effort to take account of views and suggestions of staff and members whose knowledge and experience should be of great benefit to the establishment of suitable arrangements. In order to maximise the success of the proposed arrangements, staff must play an integral part in their design and implementation and should be given a sense of ownership in the new system.

Chapter 13

Customer Service

This chapter recommends the provision of more integrated, customer-oriented services to the public through a network of joint services centres based on the joint staff/organisational structures proposed in Chapter 12.

Joint services centres

13.1 A fundamental element of the strategic review of the town and county organisations recommended at 12.26 and 12.27 would be for the authorities to carry out a thorough appraisal of their core objectives and how these are pursued. Foremost among these objectives must be the efficient provision of a high quality of service to the public. The benefits of greater cohesiveness, co-operation and co-ordination between town and county authorities can be seen to greatest practical effect in the quality of services to the public. There is now an expectation and indeed an insistence on the part of the public on the best possible quality public service. That service must be convenient, efficient and comprehensive. It must not be affected by complexities or idiosyncrasies derived from internal details of the local government system, such as the differences in functional responsibilities between different local authorities. We propose a specific model of improved public access to local services in the form of a network of joint town/county services centres. The town authorities would play a central role in the provision of an integrated public service via the joint services centres. This function should, along with the other new directions proposed in this report, constitute a major new aspect of the future role of town authorities. In the process their position as a key element in the overall local government service should be enhanced, thus complementing the deepened social, civic and community development roles proposed in Part 2.

13.2 There should be joint local services centres, offering as integrated and comprehensive a service to the public as possible. The centre would be an integrated local authority contact point for the public, (both individuals and local groups) dealing with all local government services insofar as possible, with a user-friendly, customer-oriented approach. We envisage that there will be a public office where suitably trained staff will deal with the public and respond to their queries or difficulties regardless of whether a particular matter is legally a function of the town or county authority. Through such an arrangement, the public could be offered a service covering the functional areas of both the town authority and the county council insofar as possible, in effect providing a "one stop shop" for the public. It may also be possible for such centres over time to develop the capacity to provide a focus for other public services, for example in the provision of information.

13.3 The organisational and representational arrangements recommended in Chapter 12 are a prerequisite to the joint services centre approach. In turn the joint centre should prove to be one of the most productive and the most publicly visible products of the unified local service. The creation of a joint town/county staff and operational structure will be of particular significance involving the merging, where possible, of the county council area office and the town authority office and the location of town authority staff and those of the county area office in the same building (although this may take some time to arrange in all cases). Where possible offices of other public authorities should be located conveniently to facilitate the public. As mentioned in Chapter 12, it is essential that all future local authority office development proposals should be assessed in this light, with the emphasis on serving the public and not on differences between local authorities or other public bodies. This means location of town and county staff in a single building or complex and will in many cases represent a more effective use of scarce public resources. We strongly recommend that a strategic decision should be taken now to move in this direction and to avail of all opportunities for progress as they arise. This should also apply in the case of county towns, where there are currently two entirely different local authority office centres each with separate overhead costs, but the process may be a longer term one in some of these cases.

Decentralised services

13.4 A further significant organisational issue arises. In order that the proposed integrated public service approach can yield maximum benefit, it needs to be developed and operated in the context of a decentralisation of county council services to local offices where feasible. There are already moves in this direction in some areas. These may involve a significant measure of decentralisation of the organisation to area divisions and the location of appropriate staff resources at local offices. This approach should be capable of adoption on a wider basis, subject to relevant organisational, geographic and demographic considerations. This could greatly facilitate the joint services approach which we propose. We recommend that where such decentralisation measures are being considered, the county divisional organisation should, insofar as possible, be organised around the local authority towns so as to facilitate the proposed role of town authorities in the provision of joint services. This also makes sense in demographic and communications terms, although we recognise that it may not be attainable in every case.

13.5 Staff with knowledge of the relevant services would be located in the joint centres. This would probably require an element of restructuring on the part of the county council in some cases. It would arise in any event where decentralisation of elements of the county organisation is proposed. However, to ensure a high quality integrated public service, it will be necessary to examine critically those operations which involve direct service to the public. These should be organised, not on the basis of an organisational imperative or a narrow functional approach, but from the perspective of the public and their needs. In general, members of the public should be able to transact their business at the local centre. The local centre would be geared at a minimum, to provide information and as far as possible, general advice, and accept applications or initiate transactions in most local authority matters. There should be an emphasis on eliminating or overcoming complexities in matters involving the public and minimising the need to refer persons to, for example, the county council headquarters. There would, however, still be some unavoidable limitations to the extent or depth of service which could be provided in relation to some specialised county council services. In certain cases, therefore, joint services centres would only be able to process county functions up to a certain point, particularly where special expertise, technical or legal advice or guidance might be required.

There needs to be as positive an approach as possible to identification of services for delivery on a decentralised basis. Where referral is unavoidable, the person should be given every assistance to ensure that the matter can be pursued with the minimum difficulty and inconvenience.

Human resources aspects

13.6 Human resources are a key element of the joint services centre initiative. An essential requirement is the selection of staff for the centre having suitable ability, knowledge, expertise and above all, qualities and skills necessary for dealing with the public in a customer-oriented way. Appropriate training and staff development is an essential ingredient for the success of the proposed approach. It is particularly necessary to ensure an overall ethos of customer-service and to ensure that this is reflected in the delivery of services. As in the case of other proposals for new departures, involvement of staff as early and as fully as possible in the formulation and implementation of arrangements is desirable. This will help to utilise the knowledge of staff and maximise their commitment. Attention should also be given to other important aspects of the proposed centres, such as the provision of adequate standards of accommodation and facilities. It is likely that staff requirements for the proposed centres, could be met largely through economies of scale resulting from combining the town and county personnel and the requirements which would arise in any event from upgrading of county council area offices. However, it is not possible to quantify requirements precisely until specific proposals are drawn up and costed.

IT and services to the public

13.7 The potential of information technology (IT) can be utilised to maximise the depth of service provided through the local joint office particularly where detailed information or more expert advice or guidance is required. Modern telecommunications services would need to be fully utilised so that where information or advice cannot be provided by local staff, there is ready access to sources of information e.g. county council headquarters. It should also be possible to provide more extensive direct information facilities through direct data links between the local centre and the county council headquarters or other remote locations. This would, for example, enable a member of the public at the local centre to be provided with appropriate information from a central database. Local authorities have made valuable use of information technology to improve the quality and efficiency of their operations. Use of IT can enable many administrative functions, at present carried out exclusively at headquarters, to be devolved to the local offices without loss of efficiency, thus facilitating the joint services approach. This can be brought to a further stage by applying the resources of IT as an integral part of service to the public. On-going developments in IT should be utilised as far as possible to maximise the quality and range of services available at the proposed joint services centres. Applications such as expert systems might be helpful in extending the depth of advice and assistance provided locally. Upcoming developments such as integrated voice/data facilities through integrated services digital networks (ISDN) could further enhance the extent and quality of service available locally through remote communication in due course.

Services at local centres

13.8 We do not propose to attempt a definitive model of the joint services arrangement. It may be useful to develop the concept initially through pilot schemes. However, the following is an indicative list of matters which might be dealt with on a devolved basis through the town-based joint services centres:

- collection of monies in respect of housing rents/annuities, water charges; rates; refuse charges;

- road opening licences;

- water and sewerage connections;

- planning: availability of forms, literature and development plan; procedural and other advice (but submission of formal planning applications for the county area will need to continue to go direct to county council headquarters in view of the statutory procedures and time frames involved);

- licences under the 1963 Planning and Development Act, in respect of structures on or adjacent to public roads;

- housing: promotional and advisory roles in relation to social housing measures, including advice/information on loans, grant options and schemes; (provision of advice and information locally would be especially valuable for persons without ready access to transport who desire face to face advice); acceptance of applications for housing (and co-ordination between town and county housing lists); display of plans for local authority housing development and participation in the development of housing "one stop shops" as envisaged in *Social Housing - The Way Ahead*;

- roads: handling of problems/complaints involving potholes, footpaths/kerbs, public lighting, flooding, whether on urban or county council roads (there seems to be considerable public confusion as to separate town/county responsibilities for urban and national/regional roads within towns, which makes the need for an integrated local office service especially important in this area);

- application forms and explanatory leaflets relating to services generally; display of maps and plans for local authority developments in the area; availability of Register of Electors and Draft Register;

- information and advice on other services and handling/routing of complaints with a minimum of referral of the public to a separate office (although where formal/statutory procedures are involved, as in the case of planning applications, that may be unavoidable).

13.9 A further area which merits close attention is motor tax and driver licensing. As a minimum, relevant forms should be available. Acceptance of applications would, in principle, seem feasible in many cases. Further examination may be required as to whether applications could be processed and licences issued at local offices. In principle, routine renewal-type applications may well be capable of processing locally, but where queries arise or change of particulars are involved, it may be necessary to handle the application at central level. The implications of any local processing of motor tax and driving licence applications or of other changes in the system, in terms such as cost, staffing, accommodation and security, would need to be carefully considered. As motor tax is in effect a national system with the local authorities as the operating agents, changes in the system will ultimately need to be considered at that level.

Implementation

13.10 The foregoing are offered as suggestions for matters to be dealt with through the proposed joint services centres. The list is not necessarily exhaustive and is, of course, subject to more detailed assessment of implications and practical testing on a pilot basis. Such centres, if established, should also be developed on an ongoing basis in the light of future changes in the local government system, with particular regard to possible expansion of the role of local authorities in the light of the Devolution Commission's review. It is important that the proposed centres are well planned and organised as regards the services to be provided to the public and aspects such as IT, human resources, accommodation and co-ordination with the overall local service. The centres will need to be administered to a high standard and their operation monitored, particularly in the initial stages. It will also be necessary to develop public awareness of the service. The recommendations in Chapter 7 for provision of information by town authorities are relevant in this context. Consideration might also be given to use of a suitable logo.

Non local authority services

13.11 Integrated services are being developed in other areas of the public service and it is important that the development of the proposed local authority joint services centres takes adequate account of such initiatives. It may, indeed, be possible to extend the scope of the joint services centres over time though linkage with such other integrated services. Equally, care should be taken to avoid overlap or duplication. As a minimum, basic information relating to other locally-based public services should be available. The development of IT-based public information services should also facilitate this. A policy of locating various public service offices near to each other is also strongly recommended as a means of facilitating convenient access to public services.

Chapter 14

Community Linkage

This chapter contains recommendations for linkage between town authorities and communities to facilitate the proposed community-focused role and increased interaction between communities and town authorities.

Need for structured linkage

14.1 The future role of town authorities recommended in this report involves a strong community focus. This is particularly evident in the proposed involvement in development, social and civic functions, as recommended in Part 2. We consider that this role should be underpinned by a form of structured linkage with local communities. This would help to facilitate local partnerships, joint arrangements and interaction between local authorities and local interests. The linkage proposed would forge a closer bond between town authorities and local communities, help to secure for town authorities the position of community leadership which we consider to be central to their future role and enhance their status and general public profile. This would not, in any way, constrain or diminish the independent activities of local groups.

14.2 More structured linkage between town authorities and local communities would be mutually beneficial. It would facilitate support for local initiatives and provide a means of closer on-going involvement by local communities in local government matters. The strength of community identity and the initiative and spirit of self-help which exists in many places was brought to the Commission's attention during the course of its review. Such characteristics are manifested in the objectives and activities of many local, voluntary community-based groups. These can often be highly relevant to local authority programmes and it is desirable that the scope for mutual complementarity and synergy is fully exploited.

Participation in local government

14.3 Many local authorities recognise this potential and have developed links with local groups - voluntary, sectoral or even commercial - to considerable effect. This is not universally the case, however. There may sometimes be a degree of reticence on the part of local authorities to become closely involved with, or to appear to accord significant recognition to, non-local government groups. This attitude is, at times, manifested in concern that such recognition might tend to weaken the position of the elected local authorities. The view is sometimes articulated that candidature for local authority membership is the appropriate avenue through which to seek participation in local government. This approach does not, however, take due account of the extent to which, in present day circumstances, many talented, energetic and public-spirited people wish to make a contribution to areas of activity within the sphere of local government and to have an input to decisions affecting their area. It may also give insufficient recognition to the sense of frustration which committed local groups or individuals may at times experience. They can feel that the formal operation of the local government system does not allow an adequate means for expression of their views and aspirations on an on-going basis. The community-focused and customer-service oriented role proposed in this report calls for the establishment of positive means of support for a more interactive and participative approach in local government.

14.4   We are satisfied that increased linkage with relevant non-local government interests would not weaken the position of local authorities. We are convinced that the interests of local democracy will be poorly served by failure to come to terms with the aspirations and activities of people and groups at community level outside of, but often very relevant to, the formal local authority structure. At national level, the involvement of the social partners is now an important element in policy formulation and implementation. It is essential to the future success of local government that its development should not be restricted to a static model conceived largely in the context of nineteenth century Britain. In order for local government in Ireland to flourish and reach its full potential in the future, it must be capable of developing fresh dimensions in keeping with thinking, aspirations and developments generally in modern society. One such dimension is the development of adequate channels and arrangements for local and community linkage. Recommendations for that purpose are set out in succeeding chapters in the light of the issues which have been raised. Some of these are already standard practice in many areas. What is now proposed is their formalisation and extension throughout the system.

Proposals for linkage

14.5   Joint meetings should be required to be held at least once per year between town authority members and representatives of appropriate local groups. The selection of these groups would be largely a matter for the local authority, subject to the selection process ensuring representation of an adequate cross-section of relevant interests and sectors. This might be expected to include: the business sector; broadly based community associations; organisations involved with particular sections of the community such as youth or the elderly; organisations involved with specific activities of relevance to the town authority's role such as local enterprise, development, heritage, tourism or other promotional activity. Variations to take account of local circumstances will no doubt arise. The groups to be represented would, themselves, need to be representative, and involved in areas of activity of significant interest to local government in the town. This could, however, include bodies whose remit is not confined solely to the town area. It will also be necessary to balance the objective of broadly-based representation with avoidance of an unwieldy structure. If appropriate representative groups do not already exist, the local authority should take a proactive role in devising a basis for representation as part of its role in helping to build community capacity as discussed in Chapter 7.

14.6   The proposed joint meetings would not inhibit the holding of ad hoc meetings, deputations or the like and would not affect specific areas of interaction with local groups in areas such as social housing. The process should provide a forum for two-way communication, giving local groups a greater awareness of the problems and demands facing local authorities and an understanding of their policies and priorities. This should help to foster a more participative, collaborative and supportive relationship rather than the "shopping list" approach which can sometimes be a feature of local groups' dealings with local authorities. Equally, the proposed meetings should provide the local authority with a valuable source of information on local concerns and aspirations to inform the development of its policies and proposals.

14.7   Relevant groups should be afforded appropriate representation on any committees which a town authority may have in relation to specific areas of activity such as tidy towns, development, tourism, heritage, cultural or social matters or other community related areas of activity, subject to constraints on numbers. This would bring the knowledge and experience of such groups to bear on the local authority's work and help to ensure that the authority and such groups are working with common purpose. This is already the practice in many areas, as is the practice of including local authority representation on various local bodies which is equally valuable in promoting co-operation.

14.8   Specific recommendations in Part 2 especially in relation to development, social and civic activities, are relevant to the strengthening of relationships between town authorities and local groups. The recommendation in Chapter 10 for a modernised system of recognised non-local authority bodies represents a parallel system for linkage between county councils and community interests in non local authority towns. As recommended with the latter, town authorities should not restrict consultation with relevant local groups to the set meetings or committee system but should maintain good lines of communication on an on-going basis.

Local authority membership

14.9   The Commission considered the possibility of representatives of relevant groups being nominated to membership of town authorities as a means of enhancing community involvement in local government. We doubt whether such a course would be the best way to build productive relationships in the context of town councils and do not recommend it at this time. The potential of the approach proposed in this chapter should be fully explored before such a relatively radical departure should be contemplated. In the course of our consultations, we noted strong opposition to the principle of admitting unelected persons to membership of local authorities. It was also stated that increase in the size of local authority membership would generally be undesirable. We note, however, that involvement of non-elected persons is a feature of the Vocational Education Committees, the proposed new education boards and recent local development structures. The issue is also likely to arise for consideration in the context of the work of the Devolution Commission and increased local authority linkage with the local development structures.

Benefits of linkage

14.10   We believe that the approach recommended in this chapter will prove very beneficial to local authorities, giving them greater leadership within their communities, greater involvement with developments in their communities and allowing them to be proactive and supportive rather than reactive to such developments. It can enhance the standing of local government and help to promote greater understanding of, interest in and support for local government. We hope that a further beneficial result would be an increased desire on the part of individuals or groups to participate in local government, either directly through local authority membership, or indirectly through participation in the community. In addition to the specific benefits envisaged, enhanced local linkage would tend to reflect practice in European countries where local democracy and devolved decision-making are very well developed. More active public participation in local government would appear to be entirely consistent with support on the part of local authorities and their representative organisations for their own relationship with central government being based on the principle of subsidiarity. A structure of linkage between town authorities and local/community interests would also constitute an appropriate parallel to the arrangements for enhanced linkage between town authorities and county councils recommended at Chapter 12.

Local development structures

14.11 A further local linkage and co-ordination issue is the question of the appropriate relationships that should be forged between the various local development groups which have emerged in recent years (county enterprise boards, LEADER groups, area partnership companies and others) and the local government system. This is, primarily, a matter for the Devolution Commission and we do not, therefore, propose to deal specifically with this issue. However, judging by the extent and depth of views expressed to the Commission during its review, particularly by elected members, the involvement of local authorities in the local development process to the fullest extent possible is seen as one of the most important current issues in local government. Our conclusions generally regarding the need to avoid fragmentation in development efforts apply where these bodies are concerned. While recognising that the local development agencies generally operate an a county-wide basis and the need to avoid unwieldy membership of such bodies, it would be desirable to consider, where relevant, the position of town authorities, especially the larger ones, in any linkage arrangements involving such agencies. Inclusion of some county representatives who are town members on such bodies, as happens already in some cases, would help to address this issue. In addition, we recommend that representatives of the local development agencies be included, where practicable, among the groups to be involved in the arrangements proposed at 14.5 and 14.7.

Chapter 15

General Financial Arrangements

This chapter considers the need for changes in the system of financial arrangements and relationships between town and county authorities.

Commission's role

15.1   The Commission's statutory terms of reference require it to submit proposals as to financial arrangements for each class of town local authority. It must be emphasised that this does not involve examination of the overall system of local government financing or the funding of town local authorities. The broader issues of local government funding have been the subject of much debate and are the subject of a separate consultancy study commissioned by the Minister for the Environment. The Commission considers its own role to be confined to financial arrangements for town local authorities, with particular reference to their financial relationships with county authorities. It is clear, however, that definitive positions cannot be adopted on many aspects of such financial arrangements at a time when the overall system of local government finance is itself subject to fundamental review. The Commission has identified matters which require attention in the light of its review. The precise measures to be taken will need to be considered in detail in the context of the overall study on local government finance.

15.2   Views noted during the course of the review regarding the local authority revenue base, both generally and in particular areas, are referred to in Chapter 11. The relationship between the level of funding available and the role of town authorities and local authorities generally, was also a recurring theme in submissions and consultations during the course of the review. It is not within our remit, however, to offer views in this regard. Indeed, our statutory terms of reference oblige us to have regard to the need to ensure that there is no avoidable increase in financial demands on the Exchequer or local authorities. This consideration is reflected in recommendations throughout this report, particularly in our concern to avoid diseconomies, loss of efficiency or fragmentation of the local authority revenue base and to promote greater cost effectiveness through, for example, a more cohesive local service.

15.3   It is important that the Commission's recommendations are not judged primarily in the context of views or aspirations relating to the level of local authority funding, although acknowledging the strong views held by many authorities in that regard. This aspect often tends to dominate thinking in relation to possible improvements in local government and to overshadow other potential developments of importance. The Commission considers that, aside from any changes in local government funding per se, there is scope for achieving greater effectiveness and efficiency in the organisation and operation of local services and more rational arrangements in relation to town/county relationships. We believe that various changes and initiatives recommended in this report can contribute significantly in that regard, including recommendations for new approaches by town authorities which are not primarily expenditure-dependant.

Current financial arrangements

15.4 The different functional jurisdictions of urban and county authorities give rise to particular financial responsibilities. The fact that both urban and county authorities have functional responsibilities in the urban areas whereas the urban authority has sole revenue-raising jurisdiction there, gives rise to financial transfers between them. Each urban authority makes a mandatory payment to the county council (known as the county demand). This is their contribution to the cost of services provided by the county council throughout the county including the urban areas (e.g. fire, library, various environmental functions, national and regional roads). A broad outline of these arrangements is given at Appendix 13.

15.5 The current system of inter-authority financial relationships was the subject of criticism in submissions and comments to the Commission in the course of its review. While at an emotive level there may be a feeling in some cases that the county demand has the effect of removing revenue from the town, it must be emphasised that it is subject to a statutory method of calculation and scrutiny by the local government auditor in every case. Moreover, the system is designed to apply a means of payment for the cost of services based on the principle that all areas must contribute a share. This concept is reasonable. While the county demand tends to be subject to criticism from the town perspective, it should be noted that many of the services involved tend to be of particular benefit to the urban areas where usage is concentrated, e.g. fire and library services. It is unlikely that an alternative method would impose as low a charge on such areas for these services, but there are also more significant fundamental questions, as outlined in succeeding paragraphs.

15.6 There seems to be a lack of understanding, not only of how the system of financial arrangements between town and county authorities operates, but what it is (or was originally) intended to achieve, viz. the apportionment of costs broadly in accordance with the ability of the different authorities to pay as indicated by rates or rates-related yield. The system originated at a time when local government funding was primarily rates based. Rates were then levied widely on all sectors (including domestic and agricultural) and a greater proportion of local authority income was funded from rates than is now the case. Further change occurred with the alterations in Rate Support Grant levels for technical and other reasons (which while largely neutral in overall terms, have an effect in determining the proportion of county-at-large charges attributable to different authorities). It is apparent therefore that there has been significant and fundamental change in the local authority revenue system from the time when the county demand mechanism was originally devised, with various non-rates related sources of income assuming greater significance.

15.7 Recommendations in this report for assignment of water and sewerage functions to county level would increase the incidence of county-at-large services, and thereby extend the proportion of town authority expenditure which is subject to transfer payments. It is questionable whether it is rational to have a very significant proportion of town authority budgets subject to such transfers. There are also some financial interactions between town and county authorities which are subject to more ad hoc arrangements, for example, where functions other than county-at-large services in a town (e.g. local roads) are discharged by one authority on behalf of another on foot of local agreements. Recommendations in this report regarding greater inter-authority co-operation and use of local agreements or joint arrangements to determine functional responsibility in the light of local circumstances, may tend to increase the incidence of inter-authority transfers under the present system.

Need to review arrangements

15.8 The points set out in 15.6 and 15.7 suggest a need to consider possible changes in the arrangements governing financial relationships between town and county authorities. However, the potential impact of extending the administrative boundaries of town authorities - which we have stated in Chapter 11 is desirable in principle - adds to the need for such a review.   The likelihood of serious financial impact arising from the extension of the functional jurisdiction of town authorities which have developed beyond the existing administrative boundaries, is emphasised at Chapter 11. In the event that a limited number of boundary extensions proceed in the short term, we have recommended that these would be on the basis of purely short-term ad hoc financial measures pending the introduction of appropriate financial arrangements (as well as clarification of any possible changes arising from the overall review of local government finance). Moreover, we have stated that a general process of boundary extensions cannot proceed on a long-term basis within the present system of financial arrangements without the possibility of creating serious financial instability in wide areas of the local government system and of progressively undermining the potential for the future development of the county.

15.9 In theory, the system of financial relationships between town and county authorities should operate in such a way that structural changes of the type mentioned at 15.8 would produce a largely neutral effect. Possible net loss of rates revenue to the county as a result of boundary extension should tend to be compensated for by increase in the contribution of the town authority to the county council's "county-at-large" services. However, it would appear that the system as it now operates cannot guarantee that this will operate satisfactorily, as evidenced by the assessments of financial impact which were carried out for the Commission. These indicated a likelihood of significant net loss to the county council in many cases. In contrast to the potential effects of the loss of significant elements of the county council's revenue base, there are also likely to be some cases where the area added to the town contains little commercial rates base, involving a danger of significant net cost to the town authority. In effect, the present system of revenue and inter-authority arrangements in relation to boundary extensions is at best uncertain and at worst threatening to the financial integrity of the system as a whole. At the same time, extension of the administrative jurisdiction of town local authorities to encompass the town proper appears to be generally regarded as an essential prerequisite for an enhanced system of town local government in the future. There is a need, therefore, for a fundamental review of the revenue arrangements and financial relationships between town and county; in essence a modern framework is needed to provide for necessary in-built adjustments, particularly in a situation where the overall system of funding is itself subject to review.

15.10 The sample studies of financial impact carried out for the Commission referred to already also lead to the conclusion that, as matters stand, separate revenue jurisdiction should not be assigned to any further town authorities. The group which carried out these assessments went on to suggest that a more unified financial structure within each county would facilitate changes in boundaries where appropriate. This should also facilitate the application of uniform financial procedures to town councils generally.

Criteria for future arrangements

15.11 The Commission considers that the system of financial arrangements should be able to accommodate the valid aspirations of town authorities to exercise appropriate functions throughout the town proper. Equally, the overall integrity and efficiency of the system of finance in the county as a whole must be safeguarded. Criteria which will need to be taken into account in this context are as follows:

- the need to maximise the combined revenue resources of town and county authorities;

- the need to ensure that the system of financial arrangements can accommodate the effects of structural changes such as boundary extensions on a long term basis;

- the desirability of greater uniformity in levels of rates/charges within counties;

- considerations such as simplicity, ease of understanding and general user-friendliness;

- the need to provide for smooth implementation of any revised system, including phasing-in periods and transitional arrangements;

- the need to ensure that an adequate link is maintained between responsibility for spending decisions and revenue raising; some options which might appear attractive from the point of view of simplicity and maximisation of revenue, could serve to weaken this link in the context of separate elected authorities having decision-making capacity in relation to expenditure;

- the need to tailor financial arrangements between town and county authorities to the overall system of local government finance; those which now apply do not seem to have adapted sufficiently to the significant changes which have occurred in the system of local government finance over the years.

15.12 A balance will need to be struck where some of these objectives conflict. New inter-authority financial arrangements can only be definitively decided in the light of proposals in relation to the overall system of local government finance. Accordingly, the definition of appropriate arrangements should form part of the next phase of the study of local government finance. Without prejudice to this examination, some possible approaches which might be considered are referred to in succeeding paragraphs. A detailed evaluation and assessment of the possible implications for local authorities generally would have to be carried out and possible alternative arrangements also looked at in the context of any possible changes in the overall system of local government finance.

More unified revenue arrangements

15.13 This option was considered in a preliminary way in relation to three counties by the group which carried out a sample financial impact assessment for the Commission. This involved apportioning the combined expenditure (1996 estimates) for all local authorities within the county (i.e. all town authorities and the county council) over the total effective county-at-large valuation, giving a standard rate in the pound. The total revenue yield would then be distributed among the authorities concerned in accordance with agreed budgets. It was concluded that a unified financial structure would facilitate structural changes such as boundary extensions, by avoiding the sort of distortions which could arise from such changes in a fragmented system. The overall local revenue resources available to local authorities would also be maximised. This system would also have the benefit of ending the apparent anomaly to the public of differences in rate levels between local authorities within the same county. It was noted, however, that it would be necessary to phase in such arrangements as there could be significant changes in rate poundage levels, depending on the extent of variation in existing levels as between the different rating authorities in the county. The extent of change in rate poundage levels is also influenced by whether service charges continue to be determined separately by each authority or a standardised level of charge applied.

15.14 The system would also need to operate in such a way as to maintain an effective link between spending and revenue-raising decisions and to ensure that this was not significantly weakened. Each of the authorities concerned would need to assess the effects of their budgetary decisions on revenue requirements. The portion of rates attributable to the town and county authorities respectively would need to be clearly identified. There would also need to be safeguards against the possibility of inordinate increases in some expenditure estimates in anticipation of change in poundage levels under the unified system. It should be emphasised, however, that subject to the foregoing points, a unified system need not diminish the fiscal independence of each individual authority in relation to their functional responsibilities since they would continue to determine independent budgets.

15.15 The foregoing system would need to be tested on a wider basis and details of the mechanism worked out. Equally, other possible approaches may warrant consideration. For example, consideration might be given to whether the county demand system could be replaced by one in which the cost of county council services in towns would be levied directly by the county council rather than being recovered via transfers from the town authorities at present. In this case calculation would be either on a single county-at-large basis or with separate charges in respect of the "county health district" expenditure and that attributable to the town area. The requirements for town authority services would be calculated separately but added for collection purposes with the county levy. We emphasise, however, that we did not have information as to the possible effects of this or other possible arrangements other than the approach looked at by the study group as set out at 15.13.

15.16 A further specific issue which should be examined in the context of the finance study is the possibility of raising local financial contributions on an ad hoc basis in respect of specific projects. This matter, which is referred to elsewhere in this report (see in particular 6.10) was suggested to us in the course of the review as a possible supplementary means of raising funding to enable desirable local projects to proceed, particularly in the context of town authorities whose formal revenue base is relatively limited. It is understood that such approaches operate in other countries, for example the United States of America. This concept could embrace different approaches ranging from a voluntary approach to a more formal type of levy. In the case of the latter it would be particularly desirable to explore the possible mechanics and implications in the context of wider issues and proposals relating to local authority finance. This matter is, it should be emphasised, an entirely separate matter from the question of alternative inter-authority financial arrangements dealt with above.

15.17 The Commission met with a representative of the consultants carrying out the first phase of the study on local government financing and indicated the sort of "internal" financial issues which had been identified in the course of our review. These will now need to be subjected to more detailed examination and comprehensive assessment of options in the context of further phases of the review of local authority finance. The foregoing material should be considered in greater detail and options tested on a sufficiently wide scale. In our view what needs to be developed is a new more unified framework for town/county financial inter-relationships which will fit in with whatever changes may be decided on for the overall funding of local authorities.

Part
5

General Matters

Chapter 16

Miscellaneous Recommendations

This chapter contains recommendations which do not come directly within specific areas dealt with elsewhere in this report.

16.1   During the course of its review a number of matters came to the attention of the Commission which, although not strictly contained within the main areas of its review, are nonetheless closely related and of sufficient significance to warrant noting for appropriate action. These matters are set out here under.

16.2   A considerable number of local authority submissions called for signature and ratification by Ireland of the European Charter of Local Self Government. We understand that examination of the implications of ratification of the Charter is nearing completion and that it is intended that ratification will be effected as soon as possible after this work is finalised.

16.3   A more meaningful title such as "administrator" has been recommended in Chapter 12 for the post of town clerk. In keeping with this, the reference to "town clerk" should also be dropped from the description of the post of city manager (currently termed "city manager and town clerk").

16.4   In accordance with the recommendation in Chapter 9 regarding town classification, the terms "borough" and "urban district" would be replaced by "town". Similarly the archaic title "county borough" should be replaced by the more meaningful reference "city" and any other references in local government which have largely lost their meaning (for example "county health district", "riding" and "poor law" valuation) should be replaced by suitable terms as part of the effort to make the local government system more meaningful to the public.

16.5   The recommendations relating to town classification in Chapter 9 are based on the need to include all existing town authorities in accordance with the provisions of the Local Government Act, 1994. It would appear that some of the smaller existing town commissioners may not aspire to exercising other than largely ceremonial functions. We recommend, therefore that a mechanism be provided whereby any small town authorities which might wish to do so could change from formal local authority status to, for example, the recognised local association model suggested in Chapter 10.

16.6   The Commission wishes to record the view of many local authority members which it met that the dual Oireachtas/local authority mandate should be eliminated. However, an opposite opinion was also expressed by some, that it can be beneficial to a local authority to have Oireachtas members on the council.

16.7 It was suggested to the Commission that a way should be provided to give local authorities a greater voice in the determination of national plans and policies. The proposals for an enhanced system of consultation with the local authority members' associations should assist in this regard.

16.8 Local authorities make contributions for courthouse maintenance, coroners and inquests, although they have no substantive role in these areas. Such contributions are a relic from ninetheenth century legislation when local authorities had a role, and we recommend their termination. This would not involve any cost to public funds, being a reallocation of existing responsibilities.

16.9 Some urban authorities have involvement in the provision of school meals under provisions dating back to the early decades of the century. The Departments of Education and Social Welfare should review whether such schemes are in fact the most effective response to current social needs. In our view local authority involvement in this area, particularly in the light of the entirely new structures proposed for the education sector, should be terminated. Similarly, local authority involvement in the payment of Vocational Education Committee pensions and in contributions for special schools and residential homes should also be terminated.

16.10 Local authorities have functions, under the aegis of the Department of Agriculture and Food, in relation to local abattoirs and knackeries. These are also subject to licence by that Department which is also responsible for meat export plants. In our view there may well be a case to terminate the local authority involvement in this area and to rationalise the current arrangements. The level of fees recoverable by local authorities, which are set centrally do not match the costs of their involvement. The Department of Agriculture should review the position as a matter of priority with a view to determining satisfactory future arrangements.

16.11 Submissions to the Commission suggested that there should be specific constitutional recognition for local government. This matter has also been raised in other contexts and it is understood that the proposal has been conveyed for consideration to the Constitution Review Group which is due to submit its full report shortly.

Chapter 17

Implementation and Future Developments

This chapter considers the implications for implementation of recommendations in this report, the appropriate framework and phasing and on-going developments including possible implications of other reviews relating to local government.

Modes of implementation

17.1 This report is submitted to the Minister for the Environment, in accordance with the Local Government Act, 1994, and it is the Minister's prerogative to determine the precise course of action to be taken in relation to the recommendations in the report. Various recommendations in the report would involve statutory implementation (e.g. local authority classification, titles and corporate status; allocation of functions and application of enactments; framework for inter-authority relationships; certain staffing, organisational and other administrative arrangements; financial relationships; criteria and procedures for possible establishment of new town authorities). In other cases (for example, some of the recommendations relating to arrangements between town authorities, county councils and non-local government groups and the method of delivery of local public services) implementation is likely to involve a combination of statutory requirements and local arrangements.

Implementation framework

17.2 In all cases, implementation will, ultimately, call for action on the part of local authorities. However, it is important, in order to ensure that satisfactory progress is achieved, that in addition to any statutory provisions, an effective framework is provided for implementation of necessary measures. This would make clear the areas of action which need to be pursued, indicate appropriate timescales and provide for monitoring, review and reporting. The Department of the Environment is the relevant agency for this purpose at central level. However, implementation of some recommendations is likely to involve adjustment of various technical aspects of the local government system - for example, arrangements in conjunction with the joint structures recommended in Chapter 12. This is likely to require consultation with local authorities to enable the most appropriate approaches at local authority level. At local authority level, the SMI should prove helpful to the development and implementation of measures in relation to particular recommendations in the report. It should provide a vehicle to focus on services to the public and on the need for appropriate joint town/county service arrangements.

17.3 Another key element of implementation is the phasing of action. Short-term action may be feasible in some cases, but in other cases implementation would be conditional on the development of new long-term arrangements. Developments on some aspects are linked to the other current reviews in

121

the local government sector, notably the review of local government finance. As recommended in Chapter 15, the important issues concerning financial relations between town and county authorities should be addressed in the context of the current review of local government finance, particularly with a view to facilitating necessary boundary alterations and also to minimise any possible difficulties affecting the structural and functional development of town local government. Some of the changes recommended will involve a process of organic development at local level; for example, the full development of joint town/county organisational arrangements and the evolution of town authorities within the single classification system recommended at Chapter 9.

17.4   Reorganisation of town local government and its development on the lines envisaged in this report will take time to complete and will need to be approached on a phased basis. It is important, however, to initiate action as soon as possible. In particular, we recommend early action in relation to the creation of a joint town/county staff structure and new arrangements for greater linkage between the elected members of town and county authorities, as recommended at Chapter 12. We consider these measures to be fundamental to the future role of town authorities and critical to provision of the most meaningful and effective service to the public. Other measures which we would see as priorities include: the definition of functions as discussed in Part 2; the initiation of action (possibly on a pilot basis) to develop the integrated local service arrangements and the system of enhanced local linkage (recommended in Chapters 13 and 14 respectively); and proposals generally in the report for action by local authorities to increase their focus on and interaction with local communities.

Future developments

17.5   Following from definitive decisions on the future arrangements for the sub-county level, local government consolidation and reform legislation should be enacted dealing with local authority structures, areas and powers. This should involve the repeal of the many pre-independence statutes on which the current system is largely based and their replacement by modern comprehensive legislation to provide a satisfactory and convenient statutory basis for Irish local government.

17.6   There should also be a process to keep the development of local government under ongoing review. Difficulties and anomalies noted in this review, many of which had developed over long periods of time during which the operating context of local government changed substantially, demonstrate the need for such on-going arrangements. Changes arising from the Devolution Commission's review could facilitate new relationships between local and central government. The latter could maintain strategic oversight and review of local government, providing guidance, support and promotion of standards, quality and performance. In this context a structure or process to facilitate the ongoing development of local government should promote a mutually supportive and complementary relationship between central and local government. Such arrangements might be capable of development through the Department of the Environment's current proposals for improved systems of consultation with the local authorities.

17.7 In the development of future policy, legislation or programmes relevant to local authority functions, due regard should be had to the potential role of town authorities, with particular reference to the role of the elected members. While the allocation of particular functions will inevitably be influenced by considerations such as scale, capacity and expertise, it is desirable that decisions are not based on unduly rigid or preconceived perceptions of local authority capacity based for example on population size. Scope should be allowed for diversity in the exercise of functions and for flexibility in the making of local arrangements. Account should be taken of the potential for town authorities to play a more active role in co-operation with the county councils through the cohesive operational arrangements recommended in this report.

17.8 The outcome of the review by the Devolution Commission is potentially significant to town local government. We feel that within the scope of our review, an important future role for town authorities has been identified. It is worth noting, however, that the report of the Barrington Committee in 1991 placed considerable emphasis for the operation of a meaningful sub-county tier of local government, on the importance of a programme of devolution of additional functions to local government, with a sufficient range of such functions being allocated to the sub-county tier. Since 1991 considerable momentum has been built up in extending local authority powers and discretion, particularly in relation to matters under the aegis of the Department of the Environment. Appendix 14 lists various matters involved. The Devolution Commission, in the formulation of its proposals on a public service-wide basis will, no doubt, take due account of the scope for assignment of appropriate functions to town authorities, having regard to their particular strengths and capacities and to the principle of subsidiarity. This would enable town authorities to further strengthen their role in personal, social and community type services. Equally, the question of further consolidation of the infrastructural and regulatory type services at county level could arise in that context.

17.9 The Commission has sought to follow a balanced approach in formulating the recommendations in this review, on the basis of the information presented or ascertained in the course of the review and through the application of analysis, judgement and collective decision-making to the best of our abilities. It should also be recognised that the particular directions taken were in certain respects inevitably influenced to a greater or lesser extent by the particular parameters - legal and practical - within which the review was conducted. For example, in various submissions and consultations during the review, the possibility of a model of sub-county local government based on a comprehensive sub-division of the county into units wider than town-only areas was raised. Our terms of reference did not allow us to recommend this approach and we are not, accordingly, expressing any view for or against such an option. We are aware, however, that such an approach was not accepted in the light of the models presented in the Barrington report and that there was particular opposition to it among town authority elected members. Nonetheless, we wish to point out that the vast majority of our recommendations would be equally applicable in the context of any such alternative structures.

17.10 We are confident that the recommendations in this report set down the basis for a successful and productive future role for town local government. This will, however, depend on a range of factors outlined in the report, notably:

- the development of the town authority role in new areas of activity;

- the development of the various linkages recommended, both within and outside the local government system;

- appropriate emphasis on the need for more cohesiveness and more customer-orientation in the organisation and delivery of services; and

- the application of a more appropriate system of financial relationships which is a prerequisite to the concordant and mutually beneficial development of town and county authorities.

Most fundamentally perhaps, the success of such development will be crucially dependant on the effort, innovativeness and commitment of the authorities themselves.

Signed:

J. Lacey (Chairman)

M. Adams

G. Cronin

K. Cullen

S. Dooley

M. O'Brien

A. O'Keeffe

D. Conlan (Secretary)

April, 1996

Appendices

Appendix 1

Outline of Main Features of the Irish Local Government System

1. There are 114 elected local authorities in five legal classes as follows -

Class of Authority	Number of Local Authorities	Membership Range
Borough Corporations	5	12
Urban District Councils	49	9-12
Town Commissioners	26	9
Town Authority Total	**80**	**744**
County Councils	29	20-48
County Borough Corporations	5	15-52
County and City Total	**34**	**883**
GRAND TOTAL	**114**	**1,627**

Historical Background

2. The present local government system is largely based on nineteenth century British legislation and all of the present structures were established or recognised within this framework. Borough corporations, although generally established in earlier centuries by royal charters, were reformed and reconstituted by the Municipal Corporations (Ireland) Act, 1840. Town Commissioners came into existence in some cases under an Act of 1828, in others under Private Acts, but generally under the Towns Improvement (Ireland) Act, 1854. Urban and rural (sanitary) authorities were created by the Public Health (Ireland) Act, 1878. Under the Local Government (Ireland) Act, 1898, these become urban and rural district councils, respectively. The latter constituted a comprehensive set of sub-units of the counties for which the county councils were established by the 1898 Act. The rural district councils were abolished by the Local Government Act, 1925, leaving the boroughs and urban districts as isolated units within the counties. Those town commissioners who did not become urban district councils under the 1878/1898 Acts remained legally isolated in terms of significantly inferior powers and functions. There has been little change in local authority structures since the 1920s apart from the creation of a few new town commissioners and abolition of some others in earlier years; and establishment of the three new counties for Dublin. Eight regional authorities were established in 1994 with mainly co-ordinating functions and members nominated by the city/county authorities. A map showing the location of town authorities is attached to this Appendix.

Local Authority Functions

3. Local authorities are multi-purpose bodies which operate subject to law. In addition to the general law relating to the local government system, specific codes apply to different services - e.g. Planning; Roads; Housing; Sanitary Services; Water Pollution; Control of Dogs; Fire Services; Motor Tax, etc. The functions of local authorities are classified into eight programme groups as follows:

(i) **Housing and Building**

Assessments of housing needs; provision of housing to meet those needs, either directly or through social housing initiatives; collecting rents; management and maintenance services in respect of housing stock; assistance to people housing themselves or improving their houses; enforcing certain housing standards and registration of private rented sector; settlement of travellers and homeless persons.

(ii) **Road Transportation Safety**

Upkeep and maintenance of roads; public lighting; traffic management; car parks; road safety education; registration and collection of motor vehicle taxation; licensing of drivers; licensing of taxis and hackneys.

(iii) **Water Supply and Sewerage**

Operation and maintenance of public water supply and sewerage schemes and the provision of services to households, commerical and industrial users; assisting private water schemes and provision of public conveniences.

(iv) **Development Incentives and Controls**

Preparation and making of development plans; deciding on planning applications; planning control; building control; promotional activities in the areas of tourism and industrial development; other community development activitiy.

(v) **Environmental Protection**

Operation and maintenance of land-fill sites; collection and disposal of waste and refuse; operation and maintenance of burial grounds; civil defence; dangerous buildings; water safety; fire fighting and fire prevention; monitoring and enforcement of pollution controls; street cleaning and litter prevention.

(vi) **Recreation and Amenity**

Operation and maintenance of a range of amenities such as swimming pools, libraries, parks, open spaces, community centres, galleries, museums, recreation centres and such like.

(vii) **Agriculture, Education, Health and Welfare**

Contributions to VECs; payment of VEC pensions; animal disease control; land drainage; payment of higher education grants; contributions to health boards and services of a social/educational nature.

(viii) **Miscellaneous Services**

Rate collection; elections; courthouse maintenance; coroners and inquests; malicious injury claims; bank and interest charges; dog control; operation of markets; abbatoirs; general administration.

4.   The county local authorities have all the above functions but some of them are not vested in urban authorities - e.g. fire, building control, emergency planning, library, national and regional roads, and motor tax functions are the responsibility of county councils in urban areas. In some cases functions legally vested in urban authorities are exercised on their behalf by the county council on foot of local agreements. The functions of town commissioners are much more limited than those of the other classes of local authority, most functions in those towns being vested in the county council.

5.   While local government structures have not significantly changed, functional responsibilities have been extensively adapted, for example, new local authority roles have grown in areas such as environment, planning, urban renewal, housing and general development while health functions have moved to specialist regional bodies. Recent legislation has made considerable progress towards defining a better match between local authority capacities and responsibilities in various functions.

Representational Role

6.   In addition to the specific statutory functions outlined above, a fundamental role of local government is representation of local communities, voicing local concerns and responding to local needs. Elected members represent their electorate over a range of public issues and thus are concerned with, for example, the operation of other public agencies within their areas, with other matters of public interest and with the general development of their areas.

Council and Executive

7.   The legal character of the local authority comprises two separate elements which share responsibility for performing local authority functions: (i) the elected members who constitute the council of the authority, who are elected for five year terms under the single transferable vote system of proportional representation (all residents over 18 years are eligible to vote) and (ii) a full-time salaried chief executive, the city/county manager.

8.   The elected members exercise what are termed "reserved functions" defined by law, comprising mainly decisions on important matters of policy and finance. The general policy role of elected members is explicitly recognised in local government law and members may also represent the views of the local community to other public bodies (see paragraph 6). The manager discharges what are termed "executive functions" - in effect the day to day running of the authority - within the policy parameters determined by the elected members. Any function which is not a "reserved function" is automatically an executive one. Apart from the policy role as expressed via the different reserved functions, members in addition have various powers in relation to the operation of the executive role which allow for oversight and direction of the affairs of the authority generally; and to give directions in certain circumstances. The manager's power to exercise the executive functions of the local authority is derived directly from statutory provisions (rather than delegation by the council). The manager also has a duty to advise and assist the elected members in the exercise of their functions. While the division of functions between elected members and the manager are clearly defined for legal purposes,

in practice policy and executive decisions are not totally divorced and the elected members and manager operate together, with the former having the pre-eminent role.

9.   The county manager is an officer of and employed by the county council; recruited by the Local Appointments Commission and appointed for a 7 year term. The manager is also manager for any town local authorities within the county.

Staffing

10.   Local authority staffing comprises administrative, clerical, professional and technical staffs together with craft and general workers. In all there were just under 30,000 local authority staff at 31 December, 1994 including part-time and temporary positions, of which 2,216 are employed by the 80 town authorities (but town commissioners staffing is negligible).

11.   Apart from specific functions related to the appointment and suspension of managers, all functions related to staffing are executive functions of the manager. Vacancies for senior administrative and professional posts are filled by public open competition, through an independent Local Appointments Commission. Vacancies for other local authority offices are filled directly by the local authority concerned in accordance with statutory regulations. Recruitment of craft and general workers is entirely a matter for the manager. Local authorities are also involved in sponsoring community employment schemes operated under the aegis of FÁS with up to 6,000 people employed in total.

12.   Town and county authorities have separate staff establishments but in practice there is a degree of integration in various respects. Since the late 1970s engineering services have for the most part been integrated. There are procedures for recruitment of clerical staff through a common pool. However, the town and county organisations operate independently.

Local Authority Finance

13.   Local authority financing is based on a combination of local income sources and Exchequer grants. The main local sources are rates on commercial and industrial property and income from services, e.g. housing loan repayments, local authority housing rents and annuities and service charges (domestic and commercial) in respect of water supplies, refuse collection etc.   The total amount of local revenue (1996 estimate) is £1,289m of which £102m relates to town authorities. Exchequer grants comprise both general grants, of which the Rate Support Grant is the most significant, and specific grants which are mainly capital in nature and relate to particular expenditure programmes such as housing, roads, water services, etc. Revenue expenditure involves overheads such as wages/salaries and other administrative costs, insurance, debt servicing and payment of statutory demands to various bodies and the cost of maintaining and operating capital facilities.

Local authority capital projects include construction of local authority houses, road construction, provision of water and sewerage facilities and in the case of county level authorities, such matters as the provision of fire, library and swimming pool facilities. These are mainly funded by State grants.

14. Priorities for State funding are determined nationally in the annual public service estimates and Public Capital Programme, having regard to the National Development Plan and EU Operational Programmes in the case of EU funded services. The distribution of funding between particular authorities is determined by way of allocations issued by Government Departments (or other relevant State agencies e.g. the National Roads Authority) for different programme areas. Expenditure on particular projects is determined by agreed budgets and scheduling, with grants paid in instalments commensurate with satisfactory progress of works.

Sources of Finance

15. The following table indicates the sources of funding of current expenditure of local authorities (1995 estimate) under broad headings, showing the amounts relating to town authorities and the latter as a percentage of overall current expenditure.

Local Authority Finance (1996 estimate) - Current

Source	£m Town LA	£m Total [1]	Towns as % of Total
Government	24	532	4.5
Services, etc.	50	418	12.0
Commercial rates	44[2]	399	8.3
	118	1,289	7.9

---

(1) Includes joint drainage boards, burial boards and other miscellaneous bodies
(2) Includes county demand £16m.

MAP OF LOCAL AUTHORITY AREAS

Buncrana

Letterkenny

Monaghan

Clones
Ballybay▲
Castleblaney

Ballyshannon▲
Bundoran

Cootehill▲
Dundalk

Sligo

Ballina

Cavan
Carrickmacross

Boyle

Ardee▲

Drogheda

Castlebar
Westport

Granard▲
Longford

Kells
Navan
Balbriggan▲

Mullingar▲
Trim

Tuam▲

Dublin

Athlone

Leixlip▲

Ballinasloe
Tullamore
Edenderry

Galway

Naas
Newbridge
Bray
Greystones▲

Loughrea▲

Mountmellick
Portlaoise▲

Athy

Wicklow

Birr

Ennis

Nenagh
Templemore

Carlow

Arklow

Shannon
Kilkee
Kilrush
Limerick

Thurles

Kilkenny

Muinebheag▲

Gorey▲

Enniscorthy

Listowel

Cashel

Tipperary
Clonmel

New Ross

Carrick-on-Suir
Wexford

Tralee

Waterford

Killarney

Mallow
Fermoy

Lismore▲

Tramore▲

Dungarvan

Midleton

Macroom
Cork
Passage West▲
Cobh

Youghal

Bandon▲

Bantry

Kinsale

Clonakilty

Skibbereen

County Boundaries	∿
County Boroughs	■
Boroughs	●
Urban Districts	○
Towns	▲

Appendix 2

Population, Expenditure and Staffing of each Local Authority

Part I - Boroughs and Urban District Councils

Local Authority	Population (Within boundary)	Environs Pop.	Total Pop. (1991)	Current* Exp. (1996 estimate)	Capital Exp. 1994	Staff (at 31/12/94)**
Arklow	7,987	-	7,987	1,948,501	1,204,891	40
Athlone	8,170	7,188	15,358	3,151,922	862,237	68
Athy	5,204	-	5,204	1,006,506	2,691,075	22
Ballina	6,563	1,604	8,167	1,579,330	579,348	33
Ballinasloe	5,793	99	5,892	1,578,040	631,179	41
Birr	3,280	776	4,056	847,507	564,979	19
Bray	25,096	1,857	26,953	4,789,736	3,307,947	84
Buncrana	3,118	1,270	4,388	948,621	825,830	16
Bundoran	1,463	-	1,463	757,913	927,566	12
Carlow	11,271	2,756	14,027	2,311,246	970,479	52
Carrickmacross	1,678	1,663	3,341	774,938	926,220	12
Carrick-On-Suir	5,143	-	5,143	1,146,107	378,975	28
Cashel	2,473	341	2,814	678,201	226,781	14
Castlebar	6,073	1,575	7,648	1,665,400	598,319	32
Castleblayney	2,029	909	2,938	363,745	101,992	13
Cavan	3,332	1,922	5,254	1,004,189	916,785	19
Clonakilty	2,576	236	2,812	744,210	197,023	8
Clones	2,094	253	2,347	449,763	148,958	11
Clonmel	14,531	1,031	15,562	4,566,963	3,543,480	91
Cobh	6,227	1,992	8,219	950,300	689,480	19
Drogheda	23,848	808	24,656	8,181,486	4,234,781	178
Dundalk	25,843	4,218	30,061	9,670,243	8,466,606	208
Dungarvan	6,920	-	6,920	1,648,255	924,639	40
Ennis	13,730	2,328	16,058	2,781,530	2,299,879	52
Enniscorthy	4,127	3,528	7,655	1,064,030	3,699,981	32
Fermoy	2,313	2,149	4,462	938,072	1,469,357	24
Kells	2,183	1,356	3,539	510,830	137,510	10
Kilkenny	8,515	9,154	17,669	3,328,485	1,560,624	97
Killarney	7,275	2,675	9,950	2,326,178	1,639,220	43
Kilrush	2,740	-	2,740	495,185	549,270	9
Kinsale	1,759	992	2,751	639,400	380,405	13
Letterkenny	7,186	3,540	10,726	2,012,570	1,055,648	47
Listowel	3,347	250	3,597	904,525	562,537	25
Longford	6,393	431	6,824	1,298,426	1,428,752	33
Macroom	2,363	-	2,363	694,704	244,974	12
Mallow	6,238	1,283	7,521	1,440,850	339,124	37
Midleton	2,990	2,961	5,951	716,315	314,765	17
Monaghan	5,750	196	5,946	1,619,165	1,186,704	43
Naas	11,141	-	11,141	1,840,730	846,960	29
Navan	3,415	8,291	11,706	1,123,399	717,701	22
Nenagh	5,525	300	5,825	1,219,192	815,193	27
New Ross	5,018	1,061	6,079	1,023,165	1,013,808	31
Skibbereen	1,892	-	1,892	399,515	141,483	8
Sligo	17,302	662	17,964	6,434,250	3,274,491	102
Templemore	2,188	137	2,325	362,300	1,290,645	10
Thurles	6,687	268	6,955	1,289,900	275,385	35
Tipperary	4,772	191	4,963	1,361,067	506,220	27
Tralee	17,225	637	17,862	5,146,450	4,795,476	106
Trim	1,784	2,401	4,185	458,500	177,992	12
Tullamore	8,622	808	9,430	1,963,431	681,610	48
Westport	3,688	-	3,688	1,167,475	558,789	26
Wexford	9,544	5,849	15,393	3,535,711	5,761,677	94
Wicklow	5,847	368	6,215	1,300,918	984,004	35
Youghal	5,532	296	5,828	1,089,758	483,113	26
Subtotal	**367,803**	**82,610**	**450,413**	**101,249,148**	**73,112,867**	**2,192**

* Excludes county demand (total £16m.)
** Staffing figures compiled from returns by local authorities to Department of the Environment

Part II - Town Commissioners

Local Authority	Population (Within boundary)	Environs Pop.	Total Pop. (1991)	Current Exp. (1996 estimate)	Capital Exp. 1994	Staff (at 31/12/94
Ardee	3,269	335	3,604	28,520	-	-
Balbriggan	5,414	2,310	7,724	54,180	-	3
Ballybay	459	697	1,156	11,720	12,656	-
Ballyshannon	2,426	412	2,838	50,175	5,000	-
Bandon	1,736	3,005	4,741	15,855	-	-
Bantry	2,777	-	2,777	21,666	-	1
Belturbet	1,223	-	1,223	13,855	-	1
Boyle	1,695	502	2,197	17,460	-	1
Cootehill	1,452	339	1,791	18,629	54,379	1
Droichead Nua	11,778	291	12,069	83,250	-	1
Edenderry	3,525	217	3,742	20,300	-	-
Gorey	2,193	1,647	3,840	32,120	1,697	-
Granard	1,221	-	1,221	13,140	-	1
Greystones	9,649	1,129	10,778	44,450	-	-
Kilkee	1,315	-	1,315	25,300	-	1
Leixlip	13,194	-	13,194	83,160	-	1
Lismore	715	380	1,095	5,580	-	-
Loughrea	3,271	-	3,271	34,100	108,075	1
Mountmellick	2,495	508	3,003	13,211	-	-
Muinebeag	2,573	127	2,700	17,255	15,903	3
Mullingar	8,003	3,864	11,867	39,744	5,714	4
Passage West	3,410	196	3,606	13,580	-	2
Portlaoise	3,618	4,742	8,360	31,385	-	-
Shannon	7,920	-	7,920	58,600	-	-
Tramore	6,064	-	6,064	24,100	-	1
Tuam	3,448	2,092	5,540	50,390	-	2
Subtotal	**104,843**	**22,793**	**127,636**	**821,725**	**203,424**	**24**
Total Town Authorities	**472,646**	**105,403**	**578,049**	**102,070,873**	**73,316,291**	**2,216**

Part III - County Councils

Local Authority	Population * (1991)	Current Expenditure (1996 estimate)	Capital Expenditure 1994	Staff (at 31/12/94)
Carlow	40,942	10,974,354	7,694,524	219
Cavan	52,796	18,773,689	9,319,566	405
Clare	90,918	31,258,052	10,544,484	670
Cork	283,116	90,788,873	67,282,686	2,151
Donegal	128,117	41,086,150	19,009,092	828
DunLaoghaire/Rathdown	185,410	52,369,200	**	1,192
Fingal	152,766	53,116,700	40,313,696	1,185
Galway	129,511	39,568,653	13,258,152	912
Kerry	121,894	41,330,500	26,679,282	903
Kildare	122,656	30,434,360	44,291,883	750
Kilkenny	73,635	24,100,400	15,207,607	464
Laois	52,314	24,672,317	10,640,848	352
Leitrim	25,301	13,563,180	6,640,715	247
Limerick	109,873	35,393,788	14,515,565	811
Longford	30,296	13,507,600	9,534,962	211
Louth	90,724	14,759,031	8,328,511	257
Mayo	110,713	36,717,533	25,268,495	923
Meath	105,370	29,223,907	10,089,537	486
Monaghan	51,293	16,014,772	9,562,982	296
Offaly	58,494	17,039,325	9,681,486	334
Roscommon	51,897	21,080,000	9,339,644	512
Sligo	54,756	15,703,150	8,348,147	348
South Dublin	208,739	57,564,700	20,847 297	1,078
Tipperary NR	57,854	17,328,381	12,158,226	447
Tipperary SR	74,918	22,496,886	8,422,180	503
Waterford	51,296	17,733,200	7,035,364	451
Westmeath	61,880	17,346,020	18,087,600	354
Wexford	102,069	27,083,600	8,699,383	555
Wicklow	97,265	26,748,213	26,300,323	538
Total	**2,776,813**	**857,776,534**	**477,102,237**	**18,382**

* including towns

Part IV - County Boroughs

Local Authority	Population (Within Boundary)	Suburbs Pop.	Total Pop.	Current Exp. (1996 estimate)	Capital Exp. 1994	Staff (at 31/12/94)
Cork	127,253	47,147	174,400	50,711,000	37,749,650	1,317
Dublin	478,389		478,389	223,866,443	77,374,826	6,421
Galway	50,853	-	50,853	16,141,400	9,113,625	283
Limerick	52,083	23,353	75,436	22,268,180	15,134,071	580
Waterford	40,328	1,525	41,853	15,035,950	11,999,351	293
Total	**748,906**	**72,025**	**820,931**	**328,022,973**	**151,373,523**	**8,894**

	Total Population (1991)	Current Expenditure (1996 estimate)	Capital Expenditure 1994	Staff (at 31/12/94)
Grand Total	**3,597,744**	**1,287,870,380**	**701,792,051**	**29,492**

Appendix 3

Local Government Act, 1994

Part X

Town Local Government

Local Government Reorganisation Commission	**53.**	(1) There shall stand established on such day as the Minister may appoint by order a body to be known as the Local Government Commission Reorganisation Commission ("the Commission").

(2) The provisions of the Fifth Schedule shall apply to the Commission .

Chairperson and members	**54.**	(1) The Commission shall consist of not more than seven members one of whom shall be the chairperson.

(2) The chairperson shall be appointed by the Minister.

(3) The members shall be appointed by the Minister and shall include -
    (a) a member of a county council,

    (b) a member of a local authority other than a county council or a county borough council,

    (c) a county manager,

    (d) a person having knowledge or experience of local authority staffing matters,

    (e) a person having knowledge or experience in the field of business, commerce or administration,

    (f) an officer of the Minister.

(4) A person who is for the time being entitled under the Standing Orders of either House of the Oireachtas to sit therein, or who is a member of the European Parliament, shall, while such person is so entitled or is such a member, be disqualified for becoming or being a member of the Commission.

(5) Nothing in this section shall affect the appointment of a person to fill a casual vacancy pursuant to article 2 of the Fifth Schedule.

Guidelines for Commission

55. (1) In this section and section 56, except where the context othewise requires, a reference to a town includes a reference to a borough (other than a county borough), an urban district, a town for which town commissioners are elected, and a town to which section 56(1)(c) applies.

(2) In the preparation of a report pursuant to section 56 the Commission shall have regard to -

(a) the need to secure maximum benefit from the operation of the local government system generally, including the representation of local Community interests;

(b) the need for effectiveness, efficiency and economy and to ensure that the best use is made of available resources in the operation of the local government system and in particular to safeguard the position of county councils as the primary units of local government;

(c) the need to ensure there is no avoidable increase in financial demands on the Exchequer or on local authorities with consequential implications for taxpayers and locally and that there is no avoidable increase in existing staff numbers and costs;

(d) community identity, civic tradition, local capabilities and capacities and the provision of a proper system of local government for towns consistent with the foregoing paragraphs; and

(e) such submissions as may be made to it pursuant to section 57.

Reorganisation report

56. (1) The Commission shall prepare and submit to the Minister a reorganisation report which shall contain proposals as to -

(a) (i) arrangements for satisfactory local government for towns in the State including the number of classes of local authority which should be established for such towns,

(ii) the general role and functions appropriate to each such class of authority,

(iii)   financial, staffing and organisational matters in respect of each such class, and

(iv)   consequential implications for county councils and the appropriate relationships between each such class and such councils;

(b) the appropriate class for each town for which there is a local authority in existence at the commencement of this Part;

(c) appropriate criteria and procedures for the establishment of a local authority in a town where there is no local authority;

(d) such other (if any) matters relating to local government as the Commission may consider relevant or as the Minister may request;

(e) the measures to be taken and the arrangements to be made (including administrative, statutory and transitional arrangements) for the implementation of the proposals.

(2) The Commission shall be independent in the performance of its functions.

Notice of review   **57.**   The Commission shall, as soon as may be after the day appointed under section 53(1), publish notice of the task it is assigned pursuant to section 56 and shall -

(a) invite submissions from the public,

(b) request each local authority to make a submission in relation to the said review, including such information and particulars and within such period, not being less than two months, as may be specified in the notice.

Work programme   **58.**   (1) The Commission shall commence operations as soon as may be after its establishment and complete its work within a period of 12 months thereafter or such longer period as the Minister may allow. The Commission shall, if requested by the Minister, submit an interim report on any particular aspect of its work.

(2) The Commission may, for the purposes of its organisation report, by notice in writing request any local authority to furnish to it such information as it may reasonably require within such period as shall be

specified in the request and a local authority shall comply with any such request.

Implementation of reorganisation proposals

59. (1) The Minister may, having considered a reorganisation report of the Commission, by regulations under subsection (2) give effect to and provide for the implementation of the proposals made therein, with or without modifications. Different regulations may be made at different times in respect of different matters to allow for the implementation of such proposals on a phased and orderly basis.

(2) Regulations under this subsection may make provision for -

(a) the constitution of specified classes of local authority, their titles, corporate status and finances;

(b) the allocation of functions under different enactments to local authorities of different classes and the application to authorities of different classes of specified enactments;

(c) the relationships between different classes of local authorities and county councils;

(d) staffing, organisational and other administrative arrangements;

(e) criteria and procedures for the establishment of a local authority of a particular class for a town for which there is no local authority in existence at the commencement of this Part; and

(f) such other measures as may be necessary for the establishment of such classes of local authority.

(3) Where it is proposed to make regulations under subsection (2) a draft of the regulations shall be laid before each House of the Oireachtas and the regulations shall not be made until a resolution approving of the draft has been passed by each such House.

(4) The Minister may by regulations under this subsection provide that any local authority in existence at the time of the making of such regulations shall be a local authority of such class as may be specified therein.

(5) Regulations under subsection (2) or (4) may contain all such provisions as appear to the Minister to be necessary or expedient for the purposes of or to give full effect to or to facilitate the implementation of the proposals or modified proposals referred to in subsection (1) and without prejudice to the generality of the foregoing such regulations may include provision for -

(a) the reconstitution of a local authority as a local authority of a class referred to in subsection (2)(a);

(b) the making and operation of transitional arrangements arising from or in relation to such implementation including the preparation of schemes by the relevant managers, to have effect in accordance with the provisions of the regulations, in relation to functions, finances, staffing, property, organisational arrangements or any other things affected by such implementation and for the transfer if such is necessary of any property, officers and employees or any other thing to a specified local authority;

(c) the adjustment of any matter or thing (including any financial adjustment) that in the opinion of the Minister will arise from the implementation of reorganisation proposals or modified proposals;

(d) any matter or thing for or in respect of which provision is made by section 16 or 17 of the Local Government (Dublin) Act, 1993, or for which provision may be made by order under section 9 or 34 of the Act of 1991 with such modifications as the Minister may consider appropriate in the particular circumstances.

(6) Regulations under this section shall have effect notwithstanding the provisions of any other enactment and every such enactment shall be construed and have effect subject to and in accordance with the provisions of the regulations.

Provision of services to Commission   **60.**   A local authority or a public authority may supply to the Commission, on such terms and conditions as may be agreed upon by the relevant authority and the Commission, any services, including services of staff, required by the Commission for the performance of any of its functions.

Appendix 4

Part I

Organisations/Persons Who Made Written Submissions to the Commission

Anglim, Councillor M.

Ardee Commercial Association

Ardee Town Commissioners

Arklow Urban District Council

Association of Municipal Authorities of Ireland

Association of Town Clerks of Ireland

Athlone Urban District Council

Athy Urban District Council

Balbriggan Town Commissioners

Ballina Urban District Council

Ballybay Town Commissioners

Ballybofey & Stranolar Chamber of Commerce & Industry

Ballyshannon Town Commissioners

Bantry Town Commissioners

Belturbet Town Commissioners

Birr Urban District Council

Boyle Town Commissioners

Bray Urban District Council

Buncrana Urban District Council

Bundoran Urban District Council

Butler, D.

Byrne MCC, Senator S.

Cahir Development Association

Cahir Tourism Association

Campbell, J.

Carlow County Council

Carlow Urban District Council

Carrickmacross Urban District Council

Cashel Urban District Council

Castlebar Urban District Council

Castleblayney Urban District Council

Cavan Urban District Council

Celbridge Community Council

Clonakilty Urban District Council

Clones Urban District Council

Clonmel Corporation

Cobh Urban District Council

Cork County Council

County and City Engineers Association

Donegal County Council

Drogheda Corporation

Dundalk Urban District Council

Dungarvan Urban District Council

Edenderry Town Commissioners

Ennis Urban District Council

Enniscorthy Urban District Council

Fermoy Urban District Council

Galway County Council

General Council of County Councils

Gorey Town Commissioners

Granard Town Commissioners

Greystones Town Commissioners

Haslam, R. B.

Kells Urban District Council

Kerry County Council

Kildare County Council

Kildare Town Twinning Association

Kilkee Town Commissioners

Kilkenny Corporation

Kilkenny County Council

Killarney Urban District Council

Killybegs Parish Development Association

Kilrush Urban District Council

Kinsale Urban District Council

Laois County Council

Leixlip Town Commissioners

Letterkenny Urban District Council

Limerick County Council

Lismore Town Commissioners

Listowel Urban District Council

Longford County Council
Longford Urban District Council
Loughrea Town Commissioners

Macroom Urban District Council
Malahide Community Council Ltd.
Mallow Urban District Council
Mayo County Council
McCullagh, M.
Meath County Council
Midleton Urban District Council
Monaghan County Council
Monaghan Urban District Council
Mountmellick Town Commissioners
Muinebeag Town Commissioners
Mullingar Town Commissioners

Naas Urban District Council
Navan Urban District Council
Nenagh Urban District Council
New Ross Urban District Council
Newbridge Town Commissioners

O'Donovan, Councillor C.
Offaly County Council

Passage West Town Commissioners
Portlaoise Town Commissioners

Quinn, P.

Russell, G. E.

Shankill Community Association
Shannon Town Commissioners
Skibbereen Urban District Council
Sligo Corporation
Sligo County Council
South Kerry Independent Alliance

Templemore Urban District Council
Thurles Urban District Council
Tipperary (NR) County Council
Tipperary (SR) County Council
Tipperary Urban District Council
Tralee Urban District Council
Tramore Town Commissioners
Trim Urban District Council
Tuam Town Commissioners
Tullamore Urban District Council
Turner's Cross Community Association

Westmeath County Council
Westport Urban District Council
Wexford Corporation
Wexford County Council
Whelan, P.
Wicklow County Council
Wicklow Urban District Council

Youghal Urban District Council

Part 11

Consultative Meetings With Various Groups

Association of Municipal Authorities of Ireland

Ballina UDC

Buncrana UDC

Cahir Development Association

Celbridge Community Council

City & County Managers Association

Drogheda Corporation

General Council of County Councils

Kildare Town Twinning Association

Kilkee Town Commissioners

Kilrush UDC

Laois County Council

Malahide Community Council Ltd.

Mallow UDC

Naas UDC

Portlaoise Town Commissioners

Tipperary UDC

The Commission also met representatives of the relevant county councils (usually the chairman and manager or assistant manager) in conjunction with meetings with the town authorities.

Appendix 5

Local Government Act, 1994

Amenities, Facilities and Services Which Local Authorities May Provide

Artistic and cultural activities

The provision of art galleries, arts centres, concert halls, museums, theatres, opera houses and the holding of artistic and cultural performances, exhibitions and events.

Sports, games and related activities

The provision (both indoor and outdoor) of playing fields, athletic tracks, swimming pools and other bathing places, sports centres, gymnasia and other facilities and the holding of sporting events.

General recreational and leisure activities

The provision of parks, gardens, open spaces, playgrounds, animals, picnic sites, viewing points, footpaths, walks, boats, piers, other landing places and marinas.

Civic improvements

The provision of street furniture, paving, clocks, statues, monuments and other features, illumination and decoration and other measures designed to upgrade the urban environment.

General environmental and heritage protection and improvement

Landscaping, the planting of trees and other flora, measures for the conservation, preservation and protection of landscapes and habitats, of buildings and other features of artistic, amenity, architectural, historic, heritage or natural interest.

The public use of amenities (both natural and man made)

The provision of access, signs, vehicle parks, safety equipment, information and refreshment facilities, sanitary accommodation, utilities, seating, shelter, and any other apparatus, equipment or anything else necessary to facilitate such use.

Appendix 6

Outline of Town Authority Activities*

Type of Activity	Activity carried out by		
	Town Local Authority	Town Local Authority with County Council Input	County Council

HOUSING AND BUILDING

LOCAL AUTHORITY HOUSING

Maintenance, repair and improvement	51	3	
Rent and annuity collection	54		
Allocation of houses	54		
Other housing management	32		1
Tenant purchase schemes	53	1	
Land acquisition	48	6	
Construction	40	14	
Planning and design	29	22	3
Site development	38	12	4
Refurbishment - remedial works schemes	40	10	4

ASSISTANCE TO PERSONS HOUSING THEMSELVES

Shared ownership scheme	4		50
House purchase & improvement loans	8		46
Mortgage allowance scheme	7		47
Private sites	40	7	7
Voluntary housing - rental subsidy scheme	3		38
Voluntary housing - capital assistance scheme	2		41
Other contributions to voluntary groups	4	1	38

ASSISTANCE TO PERSONS IMPROVING HOUSES

Essential repair grants			49
Disabled persons grants			50
Improvement works in lieu of L.A. housing	38	2	14

MISCELLANEOUS

Enforcement of standards	32	7	12
Travellers halting sites	16	3	18

ROAD TRANSPORTATION & SAFETY

ROAD UPKEEP

National primary roads	5		37
National secondary roads	4		41
Regional roads	7		42
Local roads	34	5	15

* Based on returns in 1994 from 54 boroughs/UDCs

Type of Activity	Activity carried out by		
	Town Local Authority	Town Local Authority with County Council Input	County Council
ROAD IMPROVEMENT			
National primary roads	4	1	37
National secondary roads	3	1	41
Regional roads	6	1	42
Local roads	34	6	14
ROAD TRAFFIC			
Traffic management	38	13	2
Traffic signs, signals, markings	31	16	7
Off street car parks	44	9	1
Off street car park bye-laws	37	7	2
On street parking controls	38	6	2
Removal/storage of vehicles	41	3	2
Traffic warden service	40	1	
Road safety-education/publicity	6	2	34
School warden service	43		4
Road lighting	48		
Control of roadside trees/drains	40	9	2
Temporary dwellings	47	1	
Preparation of compulsory purchase orders	40	6	1
WATER SUPPLY & SEWERAGE			
PUBLIC WATER SUPPLY			
Operation/maintenance	39	4	11
Collection of water charges	54		
Provision/improvement	31	13	4
PUBLIC/SEWERAGE SCHEMES			
Operation/maintenance of network	47	4	3
Operation/maintenance of treatment works	36	4	7
Public conveniences	53		
Provision/improvement of network	35	12	3
Provision/Improvement of treatment works	29	11	8
PRIVATE INSTALLATION			
Loans for individual installations	1		24
Grants for individual installations	2		25
DEVELOPMENT INCENTIVES & CONTROLS			
LAND USE PLANNING			
Planning applications	29	24	
Enforcement	38	14	
"Section 89" licensing - structures on/adjacent to public roads	32	20	
Statutory development plans	27	27	
Other plans	5	5	
Building regulations-commencement notices	3		50
Building regulations- Fire safety certificates	3	3	50

Type of Activity	Activity carried out by		
	Town Local Authority	Town Local Authority with County Council Input	County Council
INDUSTRIAL DEVELOPMENT			
Management of industrial estates	13	4	15
Provision of industrial sites	19	5	11
Advance factories	7	1	14
Promotion work	9	8	11
OTHER DEVELOPMENT AND PROMOTION			
Provision/management of commercial facilities	4	2	3
General promotion work	9	4	1
Tourism-promotion e.g. tourism brochures	32	6	4
Tourism-provision of facilities	23	6	12
URBAN RENEWAL - DESIGNATED AREAS			
Urban renewal projects	28	2	
Environmental improvements	28	2	
URBAN RENEWAL - OUTSIDE DESIGNATED AREAS			
Urban renewal projects	23	9	
Environmental improvements	23	10	
PROMOTION OF INTEREST OF THE LOCAL COMMUNITY			
Various	30		
ENVIRONMENTAL PROTECTION			
WASTE MANAGEMENT			
Operation of landfill sites	10	3	40
Other waste management initiatives and facilities e.g. recycling	11	7	24
Domestic refuse	40	3	11
Street cleaning	44	4	6
Trade and other waste	27	8	4
Litter prevention	46		1
Litter warden service	41	1	1
BURIAL GROUNDS			
Upkeep	29	3	11
Provision	23	2	13
SAFETY OF STRUCTURES AND PLACES			
Dangerous buildings	50	3	
Demolition of ruinous buildings	43	4	1
Dangerous places	48	4	
Water safety	21	8	17
FIRE PROTECTION			
Fire service	3		50
Fire prevention activities	6		47

Type of Activity	Town Local Authority	Activity carried out by Town Local Authority with County Council Input	County Council
ENVIRONMENTAL CONTROL			
Licensing under water pollution legislation	5	13	33
Pollution prevention and control	6	17	28
Other monitoring & enforcement (incl. water, noise poll.)	2	12	31
Oil pollution clearance	4	5	31
Environmental improvement & clean-up campaigns	34	5	10
Environmental information & awareness initiatives	30	9	10
RECREATION & AMENITY			
SWIMMING POOLS			
Provision/operation	18		12
Assistance to other bodies	19		1
PARKS, OPEN SPACES, RECREATION CENTRES			
Parks or open spaces	50	3	1
Recreation, leisure or community facilities	24	5	1
Assistance to other bodies	27	1	2
Social/community employment schemes	49	2	1
OTHER RECREATIONAL/AMENITIES			
Arts-promotion facilities, etc.	6		17
Museums	5	3	3
Theatres	6	3	1
Interpretative centres	7	2	2
Meeting facilities	16		
Other cultural, heritage, tourism, etc. facilities	17	2	
Conservation/improvement of other amenities, buildings, etc.	11	2	
Access to amenities, facilities, etc.	22		
Planting of trees, shrubs, etc.	52	2	
Derelict sites	51	3	
Assistance to local bodies e.g. Tidy Towns	22		
AGRICULTURE, EDUCATION, HEALTH & WELFARE			
School meals	26		3
Piers and harbours	3		5

Type of Activity	Town Local Authority	Activity carried out by Town Local Authority with County Council Input	County Council
MISCELLANEOUS SERVICES			
Land acquisition	41	6	
Land development	33	3	
Rate collection	50	4	
Provision/operation of markets	21		
Regulation of market/fairs	22		
Regulation of casual trading	54		

Notes:

1.   The above information is compiled from data obtained from local authorities in 1994. The Commission was not in a position to carry out specific verification. The table is intended to provide a general picture of the overall situation. The returns may reflect a degree of variation in interpretation as between authorities, particularly as regards categorisation of activities under the different columns. Certain regulatory activities of an occasional nature (e.g. bridge orders and extinguishment of rights of way) have not been included.

2.   In the case of some activities (e.g. fire and certain housing matters) only a limited number of town authorities have statutory functions.

3.   Some of the services listed as town authority activities are actually provided by private contractors to the authority.

Appendix 7

Local Authority Rented Houses at 31 December, 1994

Boroughs and Urban District Councils	Number of dwellings occupied
Arklow	347
Athlone	247
Athy	178
Ballina	323
Ballinasloe	245
Birr	148
Bray	878
Buncrana	46
Bundoran	31
Carlow	390
Carrickmacross	57
Carrick-on-Suir	344
Cashel	131
Castlebar	113
Castleblayney	88
Cavan	262
Clonakilty	61
Clones	58
Clonmel	548
Cobh	204
Drogheda	847
Dundalk	1,109
Dungarvan	358
Ennis	386
Enniscorthy	279
Fermoy	139
Kells	74
Killarney	168
Kilkenny	468
Kilrush	133
Kinsale	65
Letterkenny	152
Listowel	147
Longford	280
Macroom	79
Mallow	317
Midleton	152
Monaghan	219
Naas	200
Navan	97
Nenagh	195
New Ross	391
Skibbereen	38
Sligo	581
Templemore	94
Thurles	250
Tipperary	342
Tralee	878
Trim	47
Tullamore	310
Westport	93
Wexford	642
Wicklow	213
Youghal	228
Total	**14,827**

Town Commissioners	Number of dwellings occupied
Ardee	3
Ballybay	0
Ballyshannon	8
Bandon	7
Belturbet	5
Boyle	20
Callan	3
Cootehill	19
Droichead Nua	32
Gorey	1
Kilkee	6
Loughrea	1
Mountmellick	2
Muinebheag	6
Mullingar	6
Passage West	4
Portlaoise	7
Tuam	27
Total	**157**

County Councils	Number of dwellings occupied
Carlow	537
Cavan	660
Clare	752
Cork	2,624
Donegal	2,556
Dun Laoghaire-Rathdown	3,440
Fingal	1,687
Galway	1,546
Kerry	2,100
Kildare	1,401
Kilkenny	1,195
Laois	914
Leitrim	617
Limerick	1,251
Longford	664
Louth	409
Mayo	1,327
Meath	1,174
Monaghan	373
Offaly	639
Roscommon	641
Sligo	583
South Dublin	2,863
Tipperary NR	758
Tipperary SR	972
Waterford	627
Westmeath	599
Wexford	1,338
Wicklow	1,461
Total	**35,708**

County Boroughs	Number of dwellings occupied
Cork	7,129
Dublin	31,230
Galway	1,299
Limerick	3,193
Waterford	2,349
Total	**45,200**
Grand Total	**95,735**

Authorised Local Authority Housing Programme 1996

Borough and Urban District Councils	Authorised Starts 1996
Arklow	25
Athlone	15
Athy	14
Ballina	12
Ballinasloe	5
Birr	5
Bray	50
Buncrana	9
Bundoran	3
Carlow	30
Carrickmacross	2
Carrick-on-Suir	10
Cashel	4
Castlebar	12
Castleblayney	3
Cavan	10
Clonakilty	7
Clones	7
Clonmel	15
Cobh	16
Drogheda	40
Dundalk	36
Dungarvan	10
Ennis	27
Enniscorthy	20
Fermoy	10
Kells	15
Kilkenny	18
Killarney	19
Kilrush	8
Kinsale	4
Letterkenny	15
Listowel	11
Longford	20
Macroom	4
Mallow	18
Midleton	10
Monaghan	12
Naas	14
Navan	12
Nenagh	15
New Ross	12
Skibbereen	7
Sligo	33
Templemore	3
Thurles	10
Tipperary	8
Tralee	42
Trim	6
Tullamore	14
Westport	10
Wexford	34
Wicklow	20
Youghal	10

County Councils	Authorised Starts 1996
Carlow	30
Cavan	45
Clare	45
Cork	164
Donegal	163
Dun Laoghaire/Rathdown	180
Fingal	100
Galway	70
Kerry	80
Kildare	100
Kilkenny	45
Laois	43
Leitrim	42
Limerick	60
Longford	40
Louth	28
Mayo	91
Meath	67
Monaghan	31
Offaly	36
Roscommon	40
Sligo	30
South Dublin	135
Tipperary NR	25
Tipperary SR	50
Waterford	40
Westmeath	55
Wexford	94
Wicklow	65

County Boroughs	
Cork	170
Dublin	500
Galway	70
Limerick	80
Waterford	85

Appendix 9

Non-Local Authority Towns* With Population Over 1,000 (1991 Census)

Town	County	Population
Celbridge	Kildare	9,629
Carrigaline	Cork	6,482
Maynooth	Kildare	6,027
Ashbourne	Meath	4,411
Roscrea	Tipperary (NR)	4,231
Kildare	Kildare	4,194
Newcastle	Limerick	3,612
Roscommon	Roscommon	3,427
Laytown-Bettystown- Mornington	Meath	3,360
Portarlington	Laois	3,211
Mitchelstown	Cork	3,090
Ballybofey-Stranorlar	Donegal	2,972
Rathluirc	Cork	2,646
Clara	Offaly	2,505
Kilcoole	Wicklow	2,485
Tullow	Carlow	2,424
Dunboyne	Meath	2,392
Newtownmountkennedy	Wicklow	2,321
Monasterevan	Kildare	2,224
Castleisland	Kerry	2,207
Donegal	Donegal	2,193
Cahir	Tipperary (SR)	2,055
Blarney	Cork	2,043
Claremorris	Mayo	1,907
Carrrick-on-Shannon	Leitrim	1,858
Castlerea	Roscommon	1,822
Clane	Kildare	1,822
Rathkeale	Limerick	1,803
Kanturk	Cork	1,777
Duleek	Meath	1,718
Kilcullen	Kildare	1,664
Athenry	Galway	1,612
Newmarket-on-Fergus	Clare	1,583
Kilcock	Kildare	1,551
Bailieborough	Cavan	1,550
Carndonagh	Donegal	1,541
Moate	Westmeath	1,529
Killybegs	Donegal	1,522
Kill	Kildare	1,518
Abbeyfeale	Limerick	1,501
Rathnew	Wicklow	1,496
Thomastown	Kilkenny	1,487
Fethard	Wexford	1,431
Bunbeg-Derrybeg	Donegal	1,427
Banagher	Offaly	1,423
Blessington	Wicklow	1,408
Dunmanway	Cork	1,404
Tower	Cork	1,402
Castlecomer-Donaguile	Kilkenny	1,396
Graiguenamanagh-Tinnahinch	Kilkenny	1,395
Moville	Donegal	1,392
Castleconnell	Limerick	1,391
Mountrath	Laois	1,375
Kenmare	Kerry	1,366
Lifford	Donegal	1,359
Ballybunion	Kerry	1,346

* Excludes Cork suburbs (as per 1991 census) and Dublin area

Town	County	Population
Crosshaven	Cork	1,329
Bunclody-Carrigduff	Wexford	1,316
Kilmallock	Limerick	1,311
Millstreet	Cork	1,300
Abbeyleix	Laois	1,299
Ferbane	Offaly	1,285
Ballyhaunis	Mayo	1,282
Dunshaughlin	Meath	1,275
Dingle	Kerry	1,272
Ballaghadereen	Roscommon	1,270
Kingscourt	Cavan	1,260
Callan	Kilkenny	1,246
Enniskerry	Wicklow	1,238
Ballinrobe	Mayo	1,229
Killorglin	Kerry	1,229
Belturbet	Cavan	1,223
Swinford	Mayo	1,216
Cahirciveen	Kerry	1,213
Carrigtwohill	Cork	1,212
Crossmolina	Mayo	1,202
Oranmore	Galway	1,192
Sixmilebridge	Clare	1,191
Rathdrum	Wicklow	1,175
Ballybay	Monaghan	1,156
Portlaw	Waterford	1,151
Rathangan	Kildare	1,129
Buttevant	Cork	1,125
Dunleer	Louth	1,104
Newmarket	Cork	1,097
Gort	Galway	1,093
Rathdowney	Laois	1,092
Croom	Limerick	1,090
Raphoe	Donegal	1,090
Athboy	Meath	1,083
Tubbercurry	Sligo	1,069
Baltinglass	Wicklow	1,068
Lanesborough-Ballyleague	Longford/Roscommon	1,054
Stradbally	Laois	1,046
Dunmore East	Waterford	1,038
Patrickswell	Limerick	1,019
Portumna	Galway	1,017
Ballymote	Sligo	1,014

Appendix 10

Procedures for Establishment of New Town Authorities (Chapter 10)

- The process should be initiated and insofar as possible decided locally.

- A group of not less than 50 town electors or rate payers should be entitled to propose a town meeting (on payment of a moderate deposit) to consider the establishment of a town council for the town. It would be necessary for the area to be defined on a map.

- It should also be open to any recognised association referred to in 10.17 to likewise initiate such a proposal.

- The county council would on receipt of such a proposal make the necessary arrangements (including public notice) for the meeting.

- The manager would be required to draw up a report outlining the implications of the proposal for both the town and county. The report would take account of all relevant financial and organisational factors.

- If the meeting, attended by not less than 100 electors or ratepayers decided to go ahead with the proposal, an oral hearing would be arranged by the council at which all parties could attend.

- The county council, following consideration of the report of the oral hearing, could decide to accept the proposal or to reject it.

- Where the proposal is accepted the Minister for the Environment could give effect to it by statutory instrument. Where it is rejected there would be provision for its referral by the Minister to a body appointed under Part V of the Local Government Act, 1991, for examination and report.

Appendix 11

Local Government Towns Having Census Environs
(see detailed data in Appendix 2)

Ardee	Greystones
Athlone	Kells
Balbriggan	Kilkenny
Ballina	Killarney
Ballinasloe	Kinsale
Ballybay	Letterkenny
Ballyshannon	Lismore
Bandon	Listowel
Birr	Longford
Boyle	Mallow
Bray	Midleton
Buncrana	Monaghan
Carlow	Mountmellick
Carrickmacross	Muinebeag
Cashel	Mullingar
Castlebar	Navan
Castleblayney	Nenagh
Cavan	New Ross
Clonakilty	Passage West
Clones	Portlaoise
Clonmel	Sligo
Cobh	Templemore
Cootehill	Thurles
Drogheda	Tipperary
Droichead Nua	Tralee
Dundalk	Trim
Edenderry	Tuam
Ennis	Tullamore
Enniscorthy	Wexford
Fermoy	Wicklow
Gorey	Youghal

Appendix 12

Local Authority Towns Divided by County Boundaries (1991 Census)

Local Authority	Population within Town	Environs in own County	Environs in other County	Total Population
Athlone	8,170	6,381	807	15,358
Ballinasloe	5,793	19	80	5,892
Bray	25,096	42	1,815	26,953
Carlow	11,271	1,962	794	14,027
Clonmel	14,531	418	613	15,562
Drogheda	23,848	66	742	24,656
New Ross	5,018	912	149	6,079

Appendix 13

Outline of Financial Relationships Between Town and County Authorities (the county demand system)

The key features of existing financial arrangements between the county level and urban district councils and borough corporations can be described very broadly in terms of the relationships between functional and financial responsibilities. Current arrangements derive from a time when rates constituted the major source of local funding. The functional/financial responsibility is defined in terms of areas of charge for rating purposes, comprising three elements within a county as follows:

- "county at large" functions which are the responsibility of the county council throughout the entire county including all town areas,

- "county health district" functions which are the responsibility of the county council, in the part of the county exclusive of any urban districts or boroughs (but including any town commissioners' areas), and

- functions for which the urban authority is fully responsible within its own area.

Financial interactions between urban and county authorities arise primarily in relation to county at large functions and are currently governed by the "county demand" system. This mechanism determines the contribution to be made towards the cost of county at large services (functions exercised solely by the county council such as fire service, national and regional roads and the library service) by the different urban authorities for their areas and by the county council for the non-urban portion of the county. For this purpose the net cost of county at large services (i.e. the total expenditure on such services less receipts such as state grants in respect of such services) is calculated. The portion chargeable to the different areas of the county is determined by the application of a formula prescribed in law whereby the amount charged against each area is proportionate to the respective rates produce (including rates support grant) of each area. The amount chargeable to each urban area - the county demand - is a mandatory payment to the county council and must be included in the urban authority's annual estimates and thereby is collected as part of the urban rate. The county demand system does not apply in the case of town commissioners instead the latters' additional funding requirements are raised as an additional element (known as "town charges") to the county rate collected in the town by the county council.

The foregoing is intended only as a broad outline of the main features of the system and does not provide an exhaustive account of all the details involved. As mentioned in chapter 15, there is a range of other inter-authority payments for particular service areas.

Appendix 14

Recent Additions/Improvements to Local Government Powers and Discretion

General

Powers of general competence

- Local authorities provided with powers of general competence to act in the community interest effectively relaxing the "ultra vires" principle (Local Government Act, 1991).

Representational functions

- Local authorities empowered to represent the interests of the local community in such manner as they think fit (Local Government Act, 1991).

New bye-law making powers

- New broad bye-law making power to enable the elected members of local authorities to regulate a variety of matters and activities where they consider this desirable in the interests of the common good of the local community, without the need for ministerial consent or approval (Local Government Act, 1994).

- General powers to make bye-laws, relating to the control and regulation of casual trading (Casual Trading Act, 1995).

Roads

Licensing of taxis and hackneys

- Functions in relation to the operation and licensing of taxis and hackneys transferred from the Garda Commissioner to local authorities including, grant and renewal of taxi and hackney licences; creation and extension of taximeter areas; determination of licence fees and taximeter fares; determination of numbers of taxi licences which may be granted (Public Service Vehicles Regulations, 1995).

Speed limits

- County Councils and County Borough Corporations empowered to fix special speed limits (40/50 mph), and built-up area speed limits (30 mph), and disapply the motorway speed limit (70 mph) within their administrative counties. Town authorities have statutory consultation rights with the county council (Road Traffic Act, 1994).

Parking bye-laws

- Provision for road authorities to make bye-laws governing the types of parking controls to apply in their areas (Road Traffic Act, 1994 - provision to be commenced).

Traffic calming measures

- Road authorities empowered to provide traffic calming measures on public roads in their charge (Road Traffic Act, 1994).

Abandonment of public roads

- The power to abandon a local road devolved to road authorities (Roads Act, 1993).

Extinguishment of public rights of way

- Power to extinguish rights of way devolved to local authorities, with approval by the Minister for the Environment in the case of national or regional roads (Roads Act, 1993).

Control of unauthorised signs

- Local authorities empowered to remove (and after notifying the owner, dispose of) unauthorised signs, caravans, vehicles on public roads (Roads Act, 1993).

Cycleways

- Local authorities empowered to provide cycleways (Roads Act, 1993).

Control of skips

- Local authorities empowered to make bye-laws to regulate and control rubbish skips on public roads (Roads Act, 1993).

Temporary closure of public roads

- Local authority powers relating to the temporary closure of public roads strengthened. (Roads Act, 1993).

Housing

Various social housing schemes were devolved to local authorities from their inception as follows:

- Rental Subsidy Scheme
- Shared Ownership Scheme
- Mortgage Allowance Scheme
- Low Cost Sites
- Improvement Works in Lieu of Local Authority Housing
- Estate Management
- Capital Assistance Scheme

Provisions Relating to the Private Rented Sector (including Registration).

(Note: The functions applicable to different authorities/classes of authorities vary).

Planning, Environment and General

Building control system

- County councils, county boroughs and certain large urban authorities oversee and monitor the operation of the Building Regulations with powers of inspection, enforcement and prosecution, receipt of notifications of building work and decision on applications for fire safety certificates. (Building Regulations, 1992).

Planning controls on state development

- Powers of local authorities in controlling development by State authorities strengthened. (Local Government (Planning and Development) Act, 1993).

Local archives

- Local authority powers for the preservation and management of their archives and to make these archives available for inspection (Local Government Act, 1994).

Public library service

- New statutory basis for library authorities with broad, flexible powers. (Local Government Act, 1994).

Recreation and amenity

- Devolved, flexible powers to local authorities for the provision of various amenities and facilities. (Local Government Act, 1994).

Noise control

- New powers for local authorities to take steps to prevent or limit noise (Environmental Protection Agency Act, 1992).

Waste management

- The Waste Management Bill, 1995 will provide for a comprehensive statutory basis for local authority waste management planning functions.

Ministerial Controls Removed

Removal of controls regulations, 1993

- Requirement of Ministerial consent across a range of local government activities dispensed with, including the following:

  - Certain land disposals; extinguishment of market rights; application of certain monies under Derelict Sites Act, 1990.
  - Delegation of functions by county managers; aspects of local superannuation code and of local staff leave arrangements.
  - Burial grounds.
  - Days of town commissioners/urban district council meetings.
  - Dublin Corporation standing orders; operation of Iveagh Markets.
  - Assistance to local groups in a range of matters including swimming facilities; water safety; museums; concert halls; town planning research.
  - Appeals as to valuations under the Valuation Acts.
  - Excess expenditure over local estimate under section 11 of the Local Government (Financial Provisions) Act, 1978.
  - Local tender reception procedures.
  - Erection by a local authority of a building and related facilities for car parking, selling or leasing of a car park by a local authority, provision of assistance by a local authority to a person providing a car park.

Relaxation of controls on construction works

- Departmental controls on local authority housing construction schemes relaxed so that local authorities may now do the following:

162

- construct housing schemes without prior approval from the Department within specified unit cost ceilings
- accept tenders for schemes without Department approval where the tender is not more than 10% in excess of budget approved cost
- substitute purchase of private houses for new house "starts", at any time, without prior reference to Department.

- Controls over remedial works programme relaxed in line with relaxations on housing construction programme.

Bye-laws

- The need for Ministerial approval to various bye-laws discontinued. (Local Government Act, 1994)

Traffic management measures

- Need for road authorities to obtain Garda Commissioner consent for traffic signs removed. (Road Traffic Act, 1994).

Income from parking charges

- Need for Ministerial approval for expenditure of parking income removed.

Temporary local road closures

- Requirement to notify the Minister of temporary road closures removed (Roads Act, 1993).

Control of dogs

- Minister's involvement in general regulatory matters and sanctioning arrangements entered into by local authorities for the performance of a range of their functions by other local authorities, persons, animal welfare groups, etc., discontinued. (Dogs Act, 1992).

Burial grounds

- Removal of Ministerial involvement in exhumation licences and other controls (Local Government Act, 1994).

Parks and leisure facilities

- Various statutory controls replaced by modern flexible provisions, without Ministerial involvement (Local Government Act, 1994).

Pounds

- Removal of the requirements of ministerial sanction to dispose of a pound and apply proceeds (Local Government Act, 1994).

Personnel

- A substantial range of central controls in the personnel/staff area were removed in March, 1996.